Faith and Work Project

Rich in Good Deeds: A Biblic
 by Society, ed. Robert L. Plummer
*Healthy and Wealthy? A Biblical-Theological Response to the Prosperity
 Gospel*, ed. Robert L. Plummer

Rich in Good Deeds:
A Biblical Response to Poverty by the Church and by Society

Rich in Good Deeds

A Biblical Response to Poverty
by the Church and by Society

Edited by Robert L. Plummer

Fontes

Rich in Good Deeds:
A Biblical Response to Poverty by the Church and by Society

Copyright © 2022 by Robert L. Plummer

ISBN-13: 978-1-948048-73-6 (paperback)

Typeset by Monolateral in Minion 3, Ezra SIL SR, and Museo Sans.

Managing Editor: Jarrett Ford

Fontes Press
Dallas, TX
www.fontespress.com

Contents

Abbreviations

Am.	Amores
1 Macc	1 Maccabees
1QH^a	Hodayot^a or Thanksgiving Hymns^a
2 Bar.	2 Baruch
2 Macc	2 Maccabees
3 Macc	3 Maccabees
AB	Anchor Bible
AJP	American Journal of Philology
ANF	The Ante-Nicene Fathers: Translations of the Writings of the Fathers Down to A.D. 325
Apol.	Apology
Apol.	Apologeticus
BDAG	Bauer, Walter. *A Greek-English Lexicon of the New Testament and other Early Christian Literature.* 3rd ed. Revised and edited F. W. Danker, W. F. Arndt, and F. W. Gingrich. University of Chicago Press, 2000
Ben.	De beneficiis
BJRL	Bulletin of the John Rylands University Library of Manchester
BTNT	Biblical Theology of the New Testament
CAH	Cambridge Ancient History
CH	Church History
CIL	Corpus Inscriptionum Latinarum
Claud.	Divus Claudius
Cult. fem.	De cultu feminarum

Did.	Didache
Diogn.	Epistle to Diognetus
EGGNT	Exegetical Guide to the Greek New Testament
Ep.	Epistulae
Frag.	Fragments
Haer.	Adversus haereses
HALOT	*The Hebrew and Aramaic Lexicon of the Old Testament.* By Ludwig Koehler, Walter Baumgartner, and Johann J. Stamm. Translated and edited under the supervision of Mervyn E. J. Richardson. 4 vols. Brill, 1994–1999
HeyJ	Heythrop Journal
Hist.	Historiae
HTR	Harvard Theological Review
HTS	Harvard Theological Studies
ICC	International Critical Commentary
Inst.	*Institutio oratoria* (Quintilian) / *Institutiones* (Gaius)
Jdt	Judith
JECS	Journal of Early Christian Studies
JRASup	Journal of Roman Archaeology Supplement Series
JRS	Journal of Roman Studies
LCL	Loeb Classical Library
LNTS	Library of New Testament Studies
Maty. Lyons	Martyrdom at Lyons and Vienne
Metam.	Metamorphoses
NAC	New American Commentary
NICNT	New International Commentary on the New Testament
NICOT	New International Commentary on the Old Testament
NIDNTT	*New International Dictionary of New Testament Theology.* Edited by Colin Brown. 4 vols. Zondervan, 1983
NIGTC	New International Greek Testament Commentary
Noct. Att.	Noctes atticae
NPNF[1]	*Nicene and Post-Nicene Fathers*, Series 1. 14 vols. Edited by Philip Schaff. Buffalo, NY: Christian Literature, 1886–1889
NT	New Testament
NTS	New Testament Studies
OT	Old Testament

P.Oxy.	Grenfell, Bernard P., et al., eds. *The Oxyrhynchus Papyri*. Egypt Exploration Fund, 1898–
PNTC	Pillar New Testament Commentary
PRSt	Perspectives in Religious Studies
Ps.-Phoc.	Pseudo-Phocylides
Pud.	De pudicitia
Sat.	Satirae
SC	Sources chrétiennes
ScrTh	Scripta Theologica
SEC	Studies in Early Christianity
Sen.	De senectute
Sib. Or.	Sibylline Oracles
Sir	Sirach
Smyrn.	Smyrneans
StPatr	Studia Patristica
T. Benj.	Testament of Benjamin
T. Job	Testament of Job
Thras.	Thrasybulus
Tit.	Divus Titus
Tob	Tobit
Ux.	Ad uxorem
VC	Vigiliae Christianae
WAF	Works of Andrew Fuller
WBC	Word Biblical Commentary
WGW	Works of George Whitefield
WJE	Works of Jonathan Edwards
WJW	Works of John Wesley
WUNT	Wissenschaftliche Untersuchungen zum Neuen Testament
WW	Word and World

Contributors

DAVID A. CROTEAU, Ph.D., is Dean of the Seminary and School of Ministry at Columbia International University in Columbia, South Carolina, and Professor of New Testament. He has written several books including *Urban Legends of the New Testament, Urban Legends of the Old Testament*, and *Tithing After the Cross.*

MEGAN DEVORE, Ph.D., serves as Professor of Church History and Early Christian Studies at Colorado Christian University. Dr. DeVore has training in both Classics and theology. She has produced various articles, presentations, and chapters on theology and practice during the Patristic Era.

MATTHEW J. HALL, Ph.D., is the Provost and Senior Vice President at Biola University. He has contributed to several books and is the co-editor of *Essential Evangelicalism: The Enduring Influence of Carl F.H. Henry.*

JOSEPH C. HARROD, Ph.D., is Associate Professor of Biblical Spirituality and Associate Vice President for Institutional Effectiveness at The Southern Baptist Theological Seminary in Louisville, KY. He is the author of *40 Questions about Prayer* (Kregel, 2022) and *Theology and Spirituality in the Works of Samuel Davies* (V&R, 2019).

MICHAEL A. G. HAYKIN, Ph.D., is chair and professor of church history at the Southern Baptist Theological Seminary, Louisville, KY and the Director of The Andrew Fuller Center for Baptist

Studies. He is the author of a number of books dealing with Patristic and eighteenth-century Baptist studies and is also the general editor of a 17-volume edition of the works of Andrew Fuller (Walter de Gruyter).

J. BENJAMIN HUSSUNG is a Ph.D. candidate in New Testament under Dr. Jonathan T. Pennington at The Southern Baptist Theological Seminary, where he also serves as Executive Assistant to the Provost and Adjunct Instructor of New Testament Interpretation. His work has appeared in *Journal for the Evangelical Theological Society*, *Evangelical Quarterly*, *Calvin Theological Journal*, *Reviews of Biblical and Early Christian Studies*, *Presbyterion*, and *The Southern Baptist Journal of Theology*.

TIMOTHY PAUL JONES, Ph.D., serves as chair of the Department of Apologetics, Ethics, and Philosophy at The Southern Baptist Theological Seminary and as a teaching pastor at Sojourn Church Midtown. He is the author of several books, including *How We Got the Bible* (Rose Publishing), *Why Should I Trust the Bible?* (Christian Focus), and *A Life Like Heaven* (InterVarsity Press). Jones blogs at TimothyPaulJones.com and at TheApologeticsNewsletter.com.

DAVID KOTTER, Ph.D., is the Dean of the School of Theology and Professor of New Testament Studies at Colorado Christian University. Dr. Kotter was the co-founder and served as the Research Director of the Faith and Work Project at The Southern Baptist Theological Seminary. He has contributed to several books, including *The Bible and Money: Issues of Economy and Socioeconomic Ethics in the Bible* (Sheffield-Phoenix Press, 2020) and *For the Least of These: A Biblical Answer to Poverty* (Zondervan, 2015).

ROBERT L. PLUMMER, Ph.D., is the Collin and Evelyn Aikman Professor of Biblical Studies at The Southern Baptist Theological Seminary, Louisville, KY. Dr. Plummer is the host of the popular Daily Dose of Greek screencast and author, editor, or co-author of several books, including *40 Questions About Interpreting the Bible* (Kregel, 2010, 2021), *Beginning with New Testament*

Greek (B&H Academic, 2020), and *Going Deeper with New Testament Greek* (B&H Academic, 2016, 2020).

TODD A. SCACEWATER, Ph.D., is Assistant Professor in the College of International Studies at Dallas International University, Dallas, TX. He is the author of *The Divine Builder in Psalm 68: Jewish and Pauline Tradition* (T&T Clark, 2020) and editor of *Discourse Analysis of the New Testament Writings* (Fontes, 2020).

Preface

THE AUTHORS OF THE CHAPTERS of this book share a common commitment to the Bible as the Word of God. Likewise, they believe the Scriptures, as well as the thoughts and lives of Christians in earlier eras, can help us understand more clearly how we should think about economics, poverty, and wealth. I encourage you to glance through the descriptions of the chapters below. If one of the topics grabs your interest, start there. Also, take a moment to read through the brief biographies of the contributors on page xiii. I pray this book helps you and other Christians to be "a city on a hill" (Matt 5:14), with godly personal behavior and a prophetic economic voice in our day.

Robert L. Plummer

- Chapter 1: Ben Hussung enriches our understanding of the Bible's teaching on caring for the poor by focusing on Jesus's instructions in the Gospel of Matthew.

- Chapter 2: Todd Scacewater takes us on an exegetical journey through James 5:1–6 to demonstrate that "we must use the resources we have to love our neighbor, to treat others justly, and to resist hoarding resources for ourselves."

- Chapter 3: David Kotter brings together economic research and biblical reflection to argue that the government providing a universal basic income (UBI) to its citizens would not encourage human flourishing but instead promote sloth.

- Chapter 4: I (Rob Plummer) use popular children's literature to illustrate seven widely recognized economic principles. I argue that Christians can better promote human flourishing (and prevent both exploitation and deprivation) through understanding the modern "wisdom literature" of economics, which frequently overlaps with the Bible's teaching on wealth and poverty.

- Chapter 5: Joe Harrod shows the reader that significant early figures within the evangelical Christian tradition practiced giving alms to the poor and even viewed almsgiving as a formative spiritual discipline.

- Chapter 6: David Croteau challenges the traditional tithing model, claiming that such a model has often burdened the poor people it attempts to aid. In its place, Croteau advocates for what he calls "gospel-driven giving."

- Chapter 7: Matthew Hall mines the works of the evangelical statesman Carl F. H. Henry to help American Christians think critically about potential corrupting influences upon our economic system in an increasingly secularized world.

- Chapter 8: Michael Haykin instructs us in biblical generosity through a study of the British Baptist William Kiffen (1616–1701).

- Chapter 9: Timothy Paul Jones challenges us by showing how the second-century Christian church was known for its care of the poor. Strikingly, that benevolence served as an apologetic for the faith.

- Chapter 10: Megan DeVore also instructs us through Christian history, showing how the early Christian narrative of Perpetua's martyrdom includes a prominent theme of benefaction, a motif which has implications for the relationships of rich and poor in all ages.

1

Mercy as Jesus's Response to Poverty in Matthew's Gospel

J. Benjamin Hussung

"You can't take a shower in the sink." When I started working in data administration and grant writing at a local drug recovery center and homeless center, I didn't expect to find myself saying those words on the frontlines of homeless ministry, but when you work at a small non-profit, you often end up doing a little of everything. On this particular day, I happened to be the only male staff in the building during our weekly laundry and shower opportunity for homeless men, so when our front desk assistant rang my office—"Ben, you're going to need to come down and take care of this. Someone's trying to take a shower in the sink"—I ran downstairs to help.

In the bathroom, I found the normal line of men waiting to take a shower and then one man standing naked next to the sink, lathering himself in soap. I calmly explained to him our policy and asked him to put his clothes back on and wait in line for the shower. The man quickly escalated the conversation, and soon, the police came to ask the man to leave. At that point, he decided to pack up and go on his way.

Poverty in the United States often involves several factors. Some in poverty have simply been dealt a slew of difficult financial circumstances that resulted in them being without a home and necessities for a time. Others struggle with mental health issues and lack the resources to seek the help they need. And others are fighting various addictions that cripple their ability to function normally within society. Whether we pass someone at our interstate exit asking for money or we have a family member who is unable to make ends meet, everyone stands face to face with this reality on a relatively regular basis.

I honestly expected when I first began working in homelessness and drug recovery ministry to come out on the other side of the experience more compassionate and more willing to give and help those in need. What I often found, however, perhaps highlighted through my above experience, was that my constant confrontation with the complexities of poverty in many ways desensitized me to the very real needs faced by many in our community. My understanding of the ready access to non-profits, government programs, and other resources for those in poverty made me subconsciously question my own individual responsibility to help those in need, outside of giving money and time to those who are more equipped and more qualified to help those in poverty. So I found myself passing people on the street asking for money or food and simply reminding myself that there are ten to fifteen places within walking distance where they can get three hot meals a day or that there are plenty of warm beds for them to take advantage of in local shelters.

While there may be many resources available to those in need, I knew that my own developing callousness toward the poor seemed at odds with Jesus's own more personal approach to those in need, whether it be financial, physical, or spiritual. To put it bluntly, how would Jesus himself respond to those on the street who ask for money or food or help getting back on their feet? While Luke's Gospel tends to receive most attention related to poverty, Matthew's Gospel also addresses the issue, weaving it into its larger narrative picture of what it means to be a disciple of Jesus who pursues righteousness in our relationships, both with God and our neighbors. In what follows, I will (1) lay a bit of groundwork in discussing poverty and mercy in the Greco-Roman world, (2) trace Jesus's teaching on how to respond to poverty throughout Matthew, and (3) draw some application from Jesus's teaching for our own response to poverty today. Overall, I hope to show that Jesus calls disciples to show mercy to the poor by giving or lending resources and that by doing so disciples not only help those in need but also actively pursue righteousness.

Poverty and Mercy in the Greco-Roman World

Poverty

Any discussion of responses to poverty must begin by delineating what poverty actually consists of. David Armitage defines poverty in the first century simply as "material deprivation."[1] Within this broad definition, there lies a range from more severe cases (e.g., homelessness, no access to food) to milder cases (e.g., inconsistent income, limited access to food). In Matthew, πτωχός serves as the primary term used to refer to the poor. Matthew uses it once in a more spiritual sense (5:3) and four times in a more literal sense (11:5; 19:21; 26:9; 26:11), each of which we will discuss in more detail. As we will see, Matthew's more literal uses of πτωχός seem to reflect well Armitage's simple definition of poverty as "material deprivation."

Also of interest is the type of help that individuals or societies offered those in poverty in the first century. While some scholars have argued for an organized system of poor care by Jewish groups for those in poverty in the first century,[2] Timothy Murray argues convincingly that outside of the Essenes in Qumran, there is little first-century evidence of organized poor care by Jewish groups.[3] Rather, poor care in the first century tended to consist of "occasional, individual almsgiving."[4] For Murray, therefore, "we can no longer assume that the poor-care practices of the first Christians were modeled on the organized poor-care of Jewish groups."[5]

---

1 Clearly, defining a term such as "poverty" as it existed in the first century is a tall task with many necessary nuances. For a full discussion of Armitage's definition, see David J. Armitage, *Theories of Poverty in the World of the New Testament*, WUNT 2.423 (Mohr Siebeck, 2016), 24–48.

2 For example, see Lee Levine, *The Ancient Synagogue: The First Thousand Years* (Yale University Press, 2000), 27.

3 Murray shows that the vast majority of the evidence compiled by Levine and others for a first-century organized system of poor care among Jewish groups comes from rabbinic sources and likely does not reflect first-century practice. Timothy J. Murray, *Restricted Generosity in the New Testament*, WUNT 2.480 (Mohr Siebeck, 2018), 90–135.

4 Murray, *Restricted Generosity*, 134.

5 Murray, *Restricted Generosity*, 225.

Instead, the early church's understanding of themselves as a "fictive family" served as the basis for the church's unique and more organized form of poor care in the first century.[6]

Matthew's presentation of poor care seems less focused on the mutual responsibilities of the "fictive family" and more centered upon Jesus's view of mercy and the inbreaking of God's own kingdom into the world. While speaking more broadly of the New Testament's approach to poverty, Armitage captures well this connection between the alleviation of poverty and God's kingdom:

> It has been argued, in relation to the wider Jewish context, that NT construals of poverty do not depart significantly from the formative traditions of the Hebrew Bible, in which an emphasis on the goodness of material creation entails the intrinsic grievousness of poverty, and in which the existence of poverty is ultimately consequent on creation's brokenness—a correlate of human transgression. Turning away from transgression entails care for the vulnerable, in hope that a decisive reversal in favor of the people of God (sometimes themselves characterized as "the poor") will be brought about by divine initiative. The distinctiveness of NT poverty discourse within late Second Temple Judaism is centered on the inauguration of that reversal, announced in the mission of Jesus, and ratified by his resurrection. This points to a future in which the curse will no longer be operative, and in which the human *telos* of embodied life oriented towards God, sharing with others in God's material blessings, can be realized. Life in the present, on this basis, is still "life in the time of poverty," but signs of the coming reversal are to be expected, especially within the believing community.[7]

In Matthew, the poor care that Jesus calls disciples to, like his own healing of the sick, serves as a harbinger of God's kingdom. This is why "the good news" told to "the poor" (11:5) is actually *good*

---

6 Murray, *Restricted Generosity*, 224–225.

7 Armitage, *Theories of Poverty*, 247.

news for them: the breaking in of God's kingdom into our world through Jesus has rung the death knell of poverty.[8] Even though the kingdom is inaugurated but not yet fully realized, we as disciples affirm and participate in its coming by following Jesus's teaching and embodying his constant response to those in need.

Mercy

Matthew's conception of mercy (ἔλεος) flows directly from the Old Testament. Ἔλεος occurs well over 350 times in the LXX, often translating חֶסֶד (with חָנַן and רָחַם also represented). Put most simply, mercy in the Old Testament refers to compassion expressed in action benefiting those in need, with God most often the one showing mercy.[9] This understanding of mercy moves beyond the typical Greco-Roman understanding of mercy as either a political tool to be used or an emotion to be avoided. The Stoics, for example, often distinguished between *clementia* as leniency in punishment and *misericordia* as the emotion of pity or compassion. Seneca writes in *De clementia* 2.5.4,

> Pity [*misericordia*] is the sorrow of the mind brought about by the sight of the distress of others, or sadness caused by the ills of others which it believes come undeservedly. But no sorrow befalls the wise man; his mind is serene, and nothing can happen to becloud it. Nothing, too, so much befits a man as superiority of mind; but the mind cannot at the same time be superior and sad.[10]

While mercy could be understood as a virtue in a colder political sense, the emotional aspects of mercy—compassion and

---

8 Unless otherwise noted, all biblical quotations come from the *Christian Standard Bible*.

9 See, e.g., Gen 43:14; Deut 13:18; Josh 11:20; Ps 51:1; Isa 60:10; Jdt 13:14; 1 Macc 13:46; 2 Macc 4:37; 3 Macc 2:19; Sir 2:11, 18; 5:6; 18:13; 1QH 12.30.

10 Seneca the Younger, *Moral Essays*, vol. 1, *De Providentia. De Constantia. De Ira. De Clementia*, trans. John W. Basore, LCL 214 (Harvard University Press, 1928), 438–41.

empathy for those in need—had little place in the Greco-Roman consciousness.[11]

Matthew's presentation of mercy, of course, continues this more positive Jewish trajectory, in juxtaposition to the political expediency of Greco-Roman *clementia*. In Matthew, mercy primarily consists of compassion expressed in action toward those in need. This sort of mercy centers in Jesus's own teaching and reverberates throughout the Gospel in Jesus's own posture and actions toward those in need. Jesus serves, then, as the perfect embodiment of Yahweh's mercy toward his people. The fifth beatitude in the Sermon on the Mount typifies Jesus's teaching on mercy: "Blessed are the merciful, for they will be shown mercy" (5:7). Here we can begin to see the virtue-centric nature of mercy within Matthew. The question is less what merciful acts should we perform and more *what type of merciful disciples should we become.* It becomes clear as the Gospel progresses that our mercy toward others is in some sense dependent upon God's own mercy toward us (e.g., see discussion of 18:21–35 below).

Jesus's call to his disciples to be merciful here in the Sermon begins Matthew's thematic portrayal of mercy as a key virtue of discipleship. Throughout Matthew, mercy proves to be one of the primary ways that love for neighbor is expressed (22:34–40) and even one of the "more important matters of the law" (23:23). Furthermore, through his use of Hosea 6:6—"I desire mercy and not sacrifice" (Matt 9:13; 12:7)—he juxtaposes a right understanding of the law and a wrong understanding, often espoused by the Pharisees. While the Pharisees are focused on the minutia of the law at the expense of showing love for others, Jesus shows that the law centers in love for God and love for neighbor, and this emphasis should be most clearly lived out by disciples in recognizing God's own mercy for them and then living mercifully toward others.[12]

In Matthew, we find mercy discussed directly in three primary

---

11 Bruce F. Harris, "Mercy in Its Graeco-Roman Context," in *God Who Is Rich in Mercy: Essays Presented to Dr. D.B. Knox*, ed. Peter Thomas O'Brien and David Gilbert Peterson (Lancer Books, 1986), 97.

12 W. D. Davies and Dale C. Allison, *A Critical and Exegetical Commentary on the Gospel According to Saint Matthew*, 3 vols. (T&T Clark International, 2004), 1:455.

contexts: Jesus's narrative embodiment of mercy (9:27–31, 35–38; 14:13–14; 15:21–28, 32–39; 17:14–21; 20:29–34), the disciples' own call to mercy (5:7; 6:2–4; 18:21–35), and Jesus's teachings against the unmerciful Jewish leaders (9:9–13; 12:1–8; 23:23–24). Mercy finds itself expressed in different forms throughout Matthew. Forgiveness of sins, physical healing, and giving money to those in poverty are all forms of mercy throughout Matthew, and as we will begin to see below, each of these forms of mercy are ways of pursuing the righteousness required of disciples (5:20). While *note* Jesus does not actually express mercy himself by giving money or material help to someone in poverty in Matthew (Jesus's mercy is almost exclusively expressed through physical healings and forgiveness of sins), he does teach his disciples repeatedly how to respond mercifully to those in poverty. We now turn to those passages (5:42; 6:1–4; 19:16–22; 25:31–46; 26:6–16; 18:21–35).

Poverty and Mercy in Matthew's Gospel

Matthew 5:42

Jesus discusses two types of poor care in Matthew: giving and lending. Matthew 5:42 serves as both the first mention of poor care and a sort of thesis, setting out the two ways to respond to those in poverty. Jesus says, "Give to the one who asks you, and don't turn away from the one who wants to borrow from you." Jesus's command here comes toward the end of the first major section on God's law in the Sermon on the Mount (5:17–48) and in the fifth example of Jesus's interpretation of the law within that larger section (5:38–42). In each of these six examples from the law, Jesus emphasizes the greater and more holistic righteousness required of the law (5:20), as opposed to the simply outward righteousness demonstrated by the scribes and Pharisees.

In Matthew, righteousness refers to holistic alignment with God's will and coming kingdom.[13] This fifth example, while not contradicting the *lex talionis* ("An eye for an eye and a tooth for a

---

13 Here I build off Pennington's definition of righteousness in Matthew: "Whole-person behavior that accords with God's nature, will, and coming

tooth"; Exod 21:24; Lev 24:20; Deut 19:21), provides Jesus's more righteous interpretation of this point of the law. While the *lex talionis* provides a "law of kind" or put more simply a "justice of equal measure,"[14] Jesus's interpretation focuses on the heart realities that rest within those who seek justice in this way. The *lex talionis* seeks to prevent injustice in the sense of inequitable punishment and vengeful, vigilante justice. As Jonathan Pennington writes, "There is a righteousness greater and more beautiful than self-justice—letting God be the judge and righteousness maker, the one who puts the world to right."[15]

For the disciple of Jesus, then, at a practical level, Jesus's commands may feel inequitable—letting someone wrong you more than once or giving to someone to whom you owe nothing. For the disciple, however, trust in God and his own justice motivates a deep contentment with circumstances and desire to love others, even enemies (5:43–48). As Pennington further observes, this particular example serves as a helpful illustration of the virtue-centered approach to ethics we find in the Sermon, as opposed to a more deontological approach focused on individual commands to follow:

> The command to turn the other cheek does not apply to the situation of rescuing a child from abuse, nor does the example of giving to those who beg require me to hand over the keys to my car to the homeless man who approaches me in the grocery store parking lot. This kind of literalistic interpretation not only misses the point of this exegesis (nonretaliation) but also misunderstands the nature of paraenesis or ethical teaching—it gives a vision of virtue, of how to be in the world, that accords with God's righteousness; but the working out of this in the individual's life is inevitably localized. This is wisdom.[16]

kingdom." Jonathan T. Pennington, *The Sermon on the Mount and Human Flourishing: A Theological Commentary* (Baker Academic, 2017), 91.

⁴ Craig A. Evans, *Matthew*, New Cambridge Bible Commentary (Cam- Jniversity Press, 2012), 130.

'ennington, *Sermon on the Mount*, 196.

ennington, *Sermon on the Mount*, 197–198.

For Matthew, then, Jesus's interpretation of the *lex talionis* calls his disciples not to rigidly follow these commands as laws without exception but to trust in God's own justice in such a way that their own lives are marked by an inner contentment that expresses itself in mercy. In other words, as disciples trust in God, they are freed to be wronged but not pursue retaliation (i.e., forgiveness) or to be asked for money that is not owed and to give it freely (i.e., generosity). While not explicitly called mercy in these texts, each of these examples expresses a way of compassionately acting toward someone in need, whether that is someone who has wronged you and needs forgiveness or someone who is poor and needs money or a loan. For Jesus, therefore, giving to those in need should be the natural expression of the disciple's heart, holistically aligned with God's will and coming kingdom. Now we turn to the way that Jesus discusses these two types of poor care laid out in 5:42— giving to the poor and lending to the poor—throughout the rest of Matthew.

Giving to the Poor

Matthew 6:1–4

At the beginning of the next major section of the Sermon, Jesus begins to discuss piety toward God (6:1–21). In this section, he outlines three examples of righteous piety toward God: giving to the poor, praying, and fasting. The section begins with Jesus's encouragement to "be careful not to practice your righteousness in front of others to be seen by them. Otherwise, you have no reward with your Father in heaven" (6:1). His first example, then, is giving to the poor:

> So whenever you give to the poor [ποιῇς ἐλεημοσύνην], don't sound a trumpet before you, as the hypocrites do in the synagogues and on the streets, to be applauded by people. Truly I tell you, they have their reward. But when you give to the poor [ποιοῦντος ἐλεημοσύνην], don't let your left hand know what your right hand is doing, so that your giving [σου ἡ

ἐλεημοσύνη] may be in secret. And your Father who sees in secret will reward you. (6:2–5)

Here Jesus contrasts the two conflicting motivations for giving to the poor. One can either give to the poor in order to gain praise from men or praise from God the Father. The giving to the poor (ἐλεημοσύνη) that Jesus discusses here is closely related to the mercy (ἔλεος) of the Beatitudes (5:7). Ἐλεημοσύνη is often used synonymously with ἔλεος (e.g., Gen 47:29; Isa 1:27), but especially in the Second Temple period, the use found here—charitable acts or almsgiving—became more common (e.g., Tob 1:3; Sir 29:12).[17] Giving to the poor was clearly mandated according to the law (e.g., Deut 15:11), yet for Jesus, this act of mercy went beyond mere law-keeping to a key component of what the righteous life looks like.[18]

As the disciple expresses mercy by giving to the poor, then, he is practicing righteousness.[19] Key to Jesus's argument, however, is the fact that if you give to the poor in a public way in order to receive the applause of other people, your giving to the poor ceases to be an act of righteousness. Righteousness is holistic alignment with God's will and coming kingdom, both inward heart motivation and outward action. Therefore, giving to the poor motivated by the applause of people creates a divide between the disciple's heart and action. The hypocrites are characterized by this division between motivation and action: right action motivated by wrong desires. The righteous disciple, though, must be holistically righteous: right action motivated by right desires.

Similar to the way that Jesus encourages disciples to trust God's ability to enact justice in Matthew 5:38–42, Jesus essentially encourages the disciples to trust in God's ability to give just rewards

---

17 Moisés Silva, "ἔλεος," in *NIDNTT*, 2:166.

18 Pennington, *Sermon on the Mount*, 213.

19 While not in the same context of giving to the poor, Mary Hinkle Edin and David Hill have made similar observations about the relationship between mercy and righteousness in Matthew. See Mary Hinkle Edin, "Learning What Righteousness Means: Hosea 6:6 and the Ethic of Mercy in Matthew's Gospel" *WW* 8, no. 4 (Fall 1998): 355–363; David Hill, "On the Use and Meaning of Hosea vi.6 in Matthew's Gospel," *NTS* 24 (1977): 107–119. Edin, e.g., writes, "To be righteous is to show mercy." Edin, "Learning What Righteousness Means," 356.

to those who practice righteousness by giving to the poor in secret. Once again, we cannot read Jesus's command here too liter-
ally. As Pennington writes, "Giving in secret is meant not as a new
prescription requiring cash-only gifts (rather than checks used for
tracking tax-deductible giving), or that when helping a homeless
person the helper must wear a ski mask lest he or she be recognized."[20] Instead, Jesus's encouragement here to give in secret is a
hyperbolic contrast with the sounding trumpet of the hypocrites.
Jesus's disciples, therefore, must become the type of people whose
hearts and actions align holistically with God's will and coming
kingdom. Giving to the poor motivated by a desire for God's reward is one key way of pursuing the righteousness required of Jesus's disciples.

Matthew 19:16–22

Situated in the middle of Matthew's fourth major narrative section,
focused on the new community of God's people (19:2–20:34), the
story of Jesus's interaction with the rich young man provides a
narrative escalation of Jesus's encouragement toward giving to the
poor in 6:1–4. After the young man asks Jesus about the "good"
he must do to have eternal life, Jesus tells him that "if you want to
enter into life, [you must] keep the commandments" (19:16–17).
The young man asks which commandments he should keep, and
Jesus responds by listing the second table of the Ten Commandments, which is more focused on outward, social relationships
(Exod 20:2–17; Deut 5:6–21), along with the command to "love
your neighbor as yourself" (Lev 19:18), which has been key to Jesus's ethic (Matt 5:43) and will prove to be even more central as
one of the greatest commandments (22:37–40). After the young
man affirms that he has kept all these commands, Jesus tells him,
"If you want to be perfect ... go, sell your belongings and give to
the poor, and you will have treasure in heaven. Then come, follow
me" (19:20–21). The young man, of course, leaves Jesus, grieved
because of his wealth.

Jesus's command includes a call to be "perfect [τέλειος]," or

---

20 Pennington, *Sermon on the Mount*, 215.

"whole." Directly before Jesus's teaching in the Sermon on giving
to the poor (6:1–4), he calls disciples to "be perfect, therefore, as
your heavenly Father is perfect" (5:48). This wholeness does not
refer to moral perfection but wholeness of person. In other words,
to be whole means that your heart and actions—both your inward
and outward person—are aligned.[21] The young man, though he
has generally kept the law, is not "whole" because there is division between his heart and action. While he has avoided the major sins outlined by Jesus (i.e., murder, adultery, stealing, bearing
false witness) and has certainly in some ways loved his neighbor
as himself, perhaps even giving to the poor in ways that align with
Jesus's commands in 6:1–4, the young man is unable to follow Jesus's command and give all of his belongings to the poor and follow him. This response to Jesus evinces a heart that does not fully
trust God—a man who is trying to serve two masters (6:24). As
R. T. France writes, "To follow [Jesus's command] will place this
self-sufficient young man in the same position as the birds and the
flowers in 6:25–32, depending directly on the provision of a heavenly Father for the essentials of life."[22]

Therefore, while the young man may keep the law outward-
ly, his law-keeping does not flow from full trust in God and a desire for God's reward—"treasure in heaven"—as Jesus also outlines
in 6:1–4. And while Jesus may not call everyone to this extreme
expression of mercy through poor care, he does call everyone to
holistic discipleship—to come and follow him in the entirety of
their person. In other words, one's care for the poor—whether that
means donating all your resources or a portion of them—must be
motivated by full trust in God and a desire for "treasure in heaven,"
along with true love for neighbor.

Matthew 25:31–46

At the end of Jesus's final discourse, which focuses on judgment

---

21 Once again, Pennington is helpful here in his extended discussion of
wholeness in the Sermon and throughout Matthew as a whole. See Pennington,
Sermon on the Mount, 69–85.

22 R. T. France, *The Gospel of Matthew*, NICNT (Eerdmans, 2007), 735.

(23:1–25:46), Jesus tells the parable of the sheep and the goats (23:31–46). All nations will be gathered for judgment, and the king will separate them into sheep, who inherit the kingdom, and goats, who are sent to eternal fire. The basis for this judgment seems to be their response to those in need: "For I was hungry and you gave me something to eat; I was thirsty and you gave me something to drink; I was a stranger and you took me in; I was naked and you clothed me; I was sick and you took care of me; I was in prison and you visited me" (25:35–36). While the first four circumstances certainly represent symptoms of poverty as "material deprivation," the last two—sickness and imprisonment—nevertheless often went hand-in-hand with poverty in the ancient world. *yes*

One key question that has riddled interpreters for millennia is the identity of those being cared for.[23] After "the righteous" ask when they saw the king in all of these circumstances, the king responds, "Truly I tell you, whatever you did for one of the least of these brothers and sisters of mine, you did for me" (25:40). Do "the least of these brothers and sisters of mine" refer to disciples of Jesus or the poor in general? Because of Matthew's references to true disciples as Jesus's brothers and sisters (12:46–50; 28:10) and especially "these littles ones" (10:42; 18:6, 10, 14), it seems best to take those in need here to refer to disciples of Jesus.

Does this parable, then, primarily refer to how disciples of Jesus are to care for other disciples, expressing their trust in Christ by caring for those who also trust in him? France observes,

> It is probably right to read "these my smallest brothers and sisters" as a description of disciples. But to draw that conclusion does not establish that the "sheep" are commended because their treatment of disciples reveals their positive attitude to Jesus himself. For the striking feature of this judgment scene is that both sheep and goats claim that they *did not know* that their actions were directed toward Jesus. Each is as surprised as the other to find their actions interpreted in that light. They have helped, or failed to help, not a Jesus recognized in his

---

23 Davies and Allison provide a helpful breakdown of interpretations throughout church history. See Davies and Allison, *Saint Matthew*, 3:428–429.

representatives, but a Jesus *incognito*. As far as they were concerned, it was simply an act of kindness to a fellow human being in need, not an expression of their attitude to Jesus.[24]

The last sentence of France's analysis is key. While this story refers primarily to care given to those of Jesus's disciples who are poor or in need, those expressing this form of mercy toward disciples do not seem to know that they are disciples and thus represent Jesus. As Murray concludes, therefore, we are not here talking primarily about a family simply taking care of its own.[25] Most clearly portrayed in 10:40–42 and 18:5, welcoming Jesus's disciples is a way of welcoming Jesus himself, but in 25:31–46, the mercy shown to disciples was not shown *because they were disciples*. Instead, those who showed mercy to disciples were simply merciful people who cared for those in need. This is why they were surprised to find out that they had actually cared for Jesus himself through his disciples.

Perhaps most importantly, Jesus calls those who show this type of care for the poor "the righteous." As we have already discussed, to be righteous is to be holistically aligned with God's will and coming kingdom. We do not see here a system of works-based righteousness in which caring for the poor is the basis of eternal salvation. Rather, for them to be "righteous," Jesus means that their actions—caring for the poor—are wholly aligned with their heart—love for and trust in God and love for neighbor. And once again, we see several themes converging. Those who trust God enough to expend their resources in care for the poor are righteous and will inherit the kingdom and reward from the Father.

Matthew 26:6–16

The story of Jesus's anointing by the woman at Bethany comes at the beginning of the climax of Matthew's Gospel, as Jesus's crucifixion is imminent. A woman comes to him and pours an entire jar of expensive perfume on his head. The disciples react with indignance: "Why this waste?... This might have been sold for

---

24 France, *Gospel of Matthew*, 958–959.
25 Murray, *Restricted Generosity*, 144–145.

a great deal and given to the poor" (26:9). At first glance, their response seems virtuous in light of Jesus's encouragement to show mercy by caring for the poor throughout the Gospel and most recently in 25:31–46. Not to mention, giving alms to the poor was often particularly encouraged during pilgrimages to Jerusalem (cf. John 13:29).[26] Jesus acknowledges their misguided and insensitive response: "Why are you bothering this woman? She has done a noble thing for me. You always have the poor with you, but you do not always have me. By pouring this perfume on my body, she has prepared me for burial" (Matt 26:10–12). As France observes, Jesus's response shows that it is "a matter of priorities."[27] Jesus is not flip-flopping on his previous encouragements to care for the poor; he's simply showing that this woman's anointing for his burial, as a symbol of his Messianic role, is of more imminent importance.

Of most interest for our present purpose is what happens right after this account. Judas Iscariot goes to the chief priests and accepts thirty pieces of silver in exchange for handing Jesus over to him (26:14–16). Once again, we find hypocrisy, or division of person, rather than holistic righteousness. While the disciples had misplaced priorities in their response to Jesus's anointing, some of them may have at least had the right heart motivation: a desire to trust God and love their neighbor by showing mercy to the poor. For Judas at least, it is clear that any feigned desire to care for the poor did not truly match his own heart, which was bent on betraying Jesus for financial gain. Matthew's account is not as explicit as John's, which tells us that Judas is the one who expressed anger at the expensive perfume being wasted and not given to the poor and even that he "was in charge of the money-bag and would steal part of what was put in it" (John 12:4–6). The juxtaposition, nevertheless, of the disciples' desire to care for the poor and Judas's greed is striking in Matthew. Even if desires seem rightly aligned on the surface, the motivations beneath the surface can often be twisted and misaligned. Jesus, however, calls his disciples to a greater righteousness, showing mercy in a way that holistically aligns with

---

26 Davies and Allison, *Saint Matthew*, 3:445.

27 France, *Gospel of Matthew*, 974.

God's will and coming kingdom, keeping the priorities of the kingdom in mind while still helping others.

Lending to the Poor

Matthew 18:21–35

At the end of Matthew's fourth discourse unit (18:1–19:1), which
focuses on the community of God's people, Peter asks Jesus how
many times he should forgive his brother (18:21). Jesus answers
with a parable about loan forgiveness, which illustrates both the
overwhelming forgiveness that disciples of Jesus have received
from the Father and the type of forgiveness they should then offer
to others. While not the primary point of the parable, we can make
a couple of important observations about lending to the poor from
the story told by Jesus.

First, there is a clear connection between compassion and mercy. After the king's servant begs the king to be patient with him,
the king "had compassion [σπλαγχνισθεὶς], released him, and forgave him the loan" (18:26–27). Later, after the servant refuses to
forgive the loan he gave to another servant, the king reprimands
him: "Shouldn't you also have had mercy [ἐλεῆσαι] on your fellow
servant, as I had mercy [ἠλέησα] on you?" (18:33). While mercy
and compassion are not necessarily equated here, it's clear that his
response of compassion and forgiveness constituted mercy. He had
an emotional response to the servant's dire situation, and as a result, he acted to alleviate his debt out of mercy.

Second, we can learn through the servant's negative example,
that lending to others and potentially forgiving debts owed to us
is an extension of God the Father's own mercy toward us. In the
parable, the king loaned an unbelievable amount of money to the
servant and then forgave that debt. The servant, on the other hand,
loaned a much more reasonable amount of money to another servant yet would not forgive the debt. An implication of this story,
therefore, is that we should seek to become disciples of Jesus who
are merciful, precisely because we have received mercy from the
Father. This type of reflective mercy may mean giving resources

to someone in poverty or perhaps giving them a loan to get back on their feet. It may even mean forgiving the loan in full if compassion and wisdom compel us to do so. The parable ends with the punishment of the unforgiving servant and a shockingly direct statement: "So also my heavenly Father will do to you unless every one of you forgives his brother or sister from your heart" (18:35). Jesus wants to be painstakingly clear to his disciples: a heart truly transformed by the Father's unfathomable mercy toward us will become more and more merciful and seek to extend the mercy of the Father to those in need.

Application and Conclusion

From this survey of Jesus's teaching on responding to poverty in Matthew, I have shown that Jesus calls disciples to show mercy to the poor by giving or lending resources and that by doing so disciples not only help those in need but also actively pursue righteousness. From Jesus's teaching, we can draw several points of application for our own response to poverty today as disciples of Jesus.

First, we should seek to show mercy holistically. As disciples of Jesus called to pursue righteousness, we should seek to align both our hearts and our actions with God's will and coming kingdom. Our response to poverty, then, should be compassion and mercy expressed by giving or even lending resources appropriately. All of this should be motivated first by our love for and trust in God—his provision for us and his promise to reward those who humbly show mercy to others with treasure in heaven (Matt 6:1–4)—and second by our love for neighbor (22:39). We are not called simply to *do merciful acts* but to *become merciful people*, whose entire lives are so saturated with God's own mercy toward us that our hearts are transformed and our actions toward others reflective of the mercy of God.

Second, we should seek to show mercy to those in poverty both personally and generously. While we should continue to support faithfully and give resources to non-profits and other organizations that are the most well-equipped to navigate the often-difficult nuances of poor care, the picture we see in Matthew's Gospel is one of personal interaction and care for those in need. Jesus cares for the sick *personally*, and his disciples should do the same with those in poverty. As those in poverty feel loved personally by *actual people* and not just by systems or organizations, the gospel can begin to become more real in their lives and Jesus's own love for them more tangible. Furthermore, our giving should be generous. Like the rich young man, our own attachment to our wealth should not keep us from being generous in the mercy we show to those in poverty (19:16–22). Clearly, there must be wisdom in this task. We never want to give resources to those in need in ways that may actually end up empowering sin in their lives or perpetuating their poverty.[28] Yet when I walk by someone on the street who is asking for food or help, my first instinct should not be to recommend them to an impersonal resource or organization but to care for them *personally* as generously and wisely as I can.

Finally, we should show mercy to those in poverty with the ultimate goal in mind—the final death of poverty at Christ's return. Jesus was right: "You will always have the poor with you" (26:11a). As long as our world remains broken by sin, we will have those in poverty to help. Yet when God's kingdom broke into the world through Jesus, signs of its final realization began to spring up: "The blind receive their sight, the lame walk, those with leprosy are cleansed, the deaf hear, the dead are raised, and the poor are told the good news" (11:54). As his disciples, Jesus calls us to join in this work of displaying the realities of the kingdom right now in our own lives and communities. As we show mercy to the poor and share the wonderful news of Christ's final reconciliation of both physical and spiritual poverty, we long for his return and for the absolute, eternal presence of God among us. On that day, "the humble will have joy after joy in the LORD, and the poor people will rejoice in the Holy One of Israel" (Isa 29:19).

---

28 For help in navigating these difficult questions, see one of the many helpful Christian resources on poor care, like Steve Corbett and Brian Fikkert, *When Helping Hurts: How to Alleviate Poverty without Hurting the Poor ... and Yourself*, rev. ed. (Moody, 2012).

2

Poverty and the Dynamic Use of Wealth in James 5:1–6

Todd A. Scacewater

THE SCRIPTURES SPEAK often about poverty and wealth.[1] They warn against the dangers of riches, admonish those who use them wrongly, denounce those who oppress the poor, command that we love the oppressed, promote diligence and saving, and advise against waste and fraud. James was particularly concerned about the dynamic between rich and poor. Paul related that, after meeting with James and the other Jerusalem apostles, they all agreed to prioritizing "remembering the poor" (Gal 2:10). That same concern for the poor arises several times in James's canonical letter. In James 5:1–6 especially, he provides powerful imagery that condemns a certain class of rich persons because of their wicked use of resources and, as a result, their oppression and unjust treatment of the poor. This passage is especially rich in its borrowing from and interaction with other Jewish teachings on rich and poor. All of these passages condemn a static hoarding of resources because of the lost potential to employ such resources dynamically for God's purposes and for the good of the poor. Reading James 5:1–6 in this way, we find some balance to other biblical teachings that warn against the perils of wealth. Specifically, James views resources as having inherent potential for benefitting the poor but only if used in dynamic ways that accord with God's purposes.

---

1 This paper is a revised version of an earlier article: Todd A. Scacewater, "The Dynamic and Righteous Use of Wealth in James 5:1–6," *Journal of Markets and Morality* 20, no. 2 (2017): 227–242. Used by kind permission of the journal editor.

James 5:1–6 in Context

James 5:1–6 is the third passage in the epistle that focuses on the rich and poor. In the first passage, 1:9–11, the poor are juxtaposed to the rich. The poor should rejoice when they are exalted in due time and should not be envious of the rich, who will fade like the flowers "in the midst of [their] pursuits" (1:11).[2] In 2:1–10, James warns not to show partiality to the rich by providing them benefits in the Christian gatherings or by humiliating the poor. The poor are specially chosen by God to be rich in faith and heirs of the kingdom (2:5). The "rich" are so called because they are those who drag the poor into court and oppress them (2:6), thereby blaspheming God's name (2:7). The goal is to "fulfill the royal law according to the Scripture, 'You shall love your neighbor as yourself'" (2:8, citing Lev 19:18). To show partiality is sin, and to break one part of the law causes one to be accountable to the whole of it.[3]

Relevant for James's concern for the poor is his persistent use of Leviticus 19 throughout the letter.[4] Leviticus 19:12–18 gives several commandments, including commands not to oppress your neighbor or keep his wages overnight (19:13), not to be partial to the poor and thereby pervert justice (19:15), not to hate your neighbor (19:17), and climactically, to love your neighbor as yourself (19:18). These concerns for wages, justice, and love of neighbor arise eminently in James 5:1–6, as we will see.

James 5:1–6 is crafted with some rhetorical skill, similarly to many other units within the letter.[5] As with other discourse units throughout the letter, 5:1–6 opens with an imperative and a noun

---

2 All translations are my own, unless otherwise specified.

3 Commentators struggle to explain James's logic here. See a fine exposition in Leonhard Goppelt, *Theology of the New Testament*, trans. Jürgen Roloff (Eerdmans, 1981), 2:206.

4 See the allusions to or quotations of Lev 19:12, 13, 15, 16, 17b, 18a, and 18b in Jas 5:4, 12; 2:1, 9; 4:11; 5:20; 5:9; and 2:8, respectively. Richard Bauckham, "James, 1 and 2 Peter, Jude," in *It is Written: Scripture Citing Scripture: Essays in Honour of Barnabas Lindars, SSF*, ed. D. A. Carson and H. G. M. Williamson (Cambridge University Press, 1988), 309; Mark Edward Taylor, *A Text-Linguistic Investigation into the Discourse Structure of James*, Library of Biblical Studies (T&T Clark, 2006), 109–111.

5 See, e.g., Taylor, *A Text-Linguistic Investigation*, 59–120.

of address: "Come now, you rich, weep by wailing" (5:1).[6] Verse 2 proceeds to give the result of some errant action of the rich: "Your wealth is rotten and your garments are moth-eaten. Your gold and silver are tarnished and their rust will be a witness against you, and their rust will eat your flesh like fire." The errant action that results in this undesirable effect is stated tersely in verse 3: "You have stored up treasure in the last days." We now see James's condemnation taking shape: the rich should weep because they have stored up treasure in the last days, which is wicked because their stored-up treasure rots, tarnishes, and rusts. That rust will be a proverbial witness against the rich on the day of judgment.

Verses 4–6 specify what exactly James means when he says they have stored up treasure in the last days. The rich have defrauded the workers of their wages and, worse yet, have used those defrauded wages to live a luxurious and exuberant lifestyle (vv. 4–5). This theft of wages results in the effective death of the workers (v. 6), whose subsistence lifestyle cannot survive lack of pay for long. The section ends with another terse, yet ambiguous, phrase that may be translated either "he does not oppose you" or "does he not oppose you?" (on which, see more below).

In sum, James condemns the rich because they have stored up treasure in the last days. Specifically, they have done so by defrauding poor workers of their wages and using those wages to engorge themselves with luxuries while their workers suffered miseries.

The Meaning of "Rich" and "Poor"

A common misconception is that the terms "rich" and "poor" in Scripture refer simply to those who have and do not have material possessions, respectively. This conception is mostly true with words translated as "rich" but is incorrect with words translated as "poor," which have a much broader semantic range that includes

---

6 William Varner has argued that James marks all of his new units with a noun of address plus an imperative or rhetorical questions. The units are 1:2–15; 1:16–18; 1:19–27; 2:1–13; 2:14–26; 3:1–12; 3:13–18; 4:1–10; 4:11–12; 4:13–17; 5:1–6; 5:7–11; 5:12–18; and 5:19–20. See William Varner, "James," in *Discourse Analysis of the New Testament Writings*, ed. Todd A. Scacewater (Fontes Press, 2020), 572–573.

socio-political, spiritual, and economic aspects. To understand
James's condemnation of the "rich" and his desire that we love and
serve the "poor," we must first understand properly what those
terms mean.

The most common Hebrew adjective to describe the poor is
ʿānî, occurring 120 times in the OT. It can refer to a person who
lacks possessions (Exod 22:25) but more so to a person who is oppressed or miserable (Pss 10:2; 25:18). Its noun form (also ʿānî)
refers to the state of misery or oppression (Gen 16:11). The word
ʿānî often carries spiritual connotations of righteousness because
they have no ability to rely on themselves but must turn to God for
recompense (Zeph 2:3; Prov 15:33; 22:4).[7] The fact that ʿānî does
not solely refer to lack of wealth is evident, for example, when it is
used to describe Moses as the most "humble/lowly" man on earth
(Num 12:3) or David (a rich king) as "poor/miserable" (Ps 25:18).

The adjective ʾebyôn occurs 61 times in the OT, mostly in the
psalms and often in parallel with ʿānî ("poor and needy"; e.g., Ps
37:14). The two terms, therefore, share a similar range of meaning. The rare adjective dāk occurs in parallel to the phrase "poor
and needy" (Ps 74:21) and simply expresses oppression (Pss 9:10;
10:18; Prov 26:28). The adjective dal similarly expresses very
broadly "low, helpless, powerless, insignificant, financially poor,
and downcast."[8] The adjective rāš is an exception, in that it appears almost exclusively in wisdom literature and refers narrowly to those who lack material possessions (e.g., Prov 13:8; 14:20;
19:7; 22:7). But even those who are rāš are still referred to in contexts of oppression because, especially in the ancient world, those
who lacked monetary means lacked socio-political power (Prov
17:5; 29:13; Eccl 5:8; Ps 82:3; 1 Sam 12:1–4).

The broad range of meaning of these Hebrew words is evident from their translation into the Septuagint. For these four
Hebrew words alone, the translators employed twelve different

---

7 Of the ʿānî, Moo says, "The poor person, helpless and afflicted by the
wealthy and powerful, calls out to God for deliverance. God, in turn, promises to
rescue the poor from his or her distress and to judge the wicked oppressor." Douglas J. Moo, *The Letter of James*, PNTC (Eerdmans, 2000), 35.

8 HALOT, s.v. דַּל (dal).

Greek terms: πτωχός ("poor"), πένης ("poor, needy"), ταπεινός ("humility"), ἀσθενής ("weakness, sickness"), πραΰς ("gentle, humble"), κάκωσις ("affliction"), ἐνδεής ("poor, impoverished"), ἐπιδεομένος ("poor, needy"), ἀδύνατος ("powerless"), ἀνήρ ἐν ἀνάγκῃ ("man in distress"), ἀπηλπισμένος ("despairing"), and ἀθυμέων ("disheartened"). As is evident from these glosses that focus less on wealth, the Septuagint translators understood that the Hebrew terms for poor were more about socio-political oppression and a powerless spiritual disposition than strictly about lack of resources.

In contrast with words for "poor," Hebrew and Greek words for "rich" express more narrowly the idea of abundance and wealth. The Hebrew verb ʿāshar means "to be rich" strictly in the sense of monetary possessions (Gen 14:23; Job 15:29; Prov 10:22), while its adjectival form ʿāshîr ("rich") similarly denotes abundance (Exod 30:15). The noun form ʿosher denotes wealth or riches (Gen 14:26; 1 Kgs 3:11; 2 Chr 1:11). Despite its strict monetary meaning, like its counterpart rāš ("poor"), the ʿāshar word group connotes in various contexts the idea of oppression and spiritual depravity. For example, in Nathan's parable, it is the "rich" man (ʿāshîr) who exploits and steals from the "poor" man (rāš). Thus, while Greek and Hebrew terms for "rich" do not strictly signify the meaning of oppression and power, they frequently do connote those ideas. Terms for "poor," on the other hand, almost always carry the idea of oppression as part of their meaning, and it is assumed that the "rich" who are wicked are the ones who oppress them. That "poor" and "rich" in the Bible are more about socio-political oppression and spiritual disposition and less about monetary possessions is recognized by many biblical scholars.[9]

---

9 E.g., Léon Roy, "Poor," in *Dictionary of Biblical Theology*, ed. Xavier Léon-Dufour, 2nd ed. (Seabury Press, 1973), 436; R. B. Edwards, "Rich and Poor," in *Dictionary of Jesus and the Gospels*, ed. Joel B. Green and Scot McKnight, 2nd ed. (InterVarsity Press, 1992), 706–707; Joel B. Green, *The Theology of the Gospel of Luke*, New Testament Theology (Cambridge University Press, 1995), 82; Leonhard Goppelt, *The Ministry of Jesus in its Theological Significance*, trans. Jürgen Roloff (Eerdmans, 1981), 84; to some extent, Bruce J. Malina, *The New Testament World: Insights from Cultural Anthropology*, 3rd rev. and exp. ed. (Westminster John Knox, 2001), 81–107.

When we encounter the "rich" and "poor" in James 5:1–6, we must avoid strictly monetary categories. The economic aspect is certainly apparent since the rich own fields and hire the poor as their laborers. But the socio-political aspect is the dominant concern here because the rich have the power to defraud the wages of the poor workers. The poor presumably have no realistic social or legal recourses because they lack the wealth, status, and prestige that would earn them such recourses in their society. The problem here in James 5:1–6 is not the possession of wealth or being rich *per se.* Rather, the problem is the wicked use of their social power and also, as we will now see, a wicked use of their resources.

The Reason for the Denunciation of the Rich

James clearly denounces the rich with prophetic language. He tells them to "weep" (κλαίω) by "wailing" (ὀλολύζω). The verb κλαίω is used throughout the Septuagint to express the weeping of those suffering God's judgment (e.g., Lam 1:1–2; Isa 15:2, 5; 33:7; Jer 8:23; Hos 12:5; Joel 1:5). The verb ὀλολύζω occurs twenty-one times in the Septuagint, always in a context of prophetic judgment.[10] The verb occurs only here in the NT. James, therefore, uses the combination of these two words from texts of prophetic judgment to denounce the rich who are defrauding the poor of their wages and hoarding their wealth for selfish gain. He says they should "weep by wailing" because of "the miseries that are coming upon you." The use of the imperfective aspect ("coming upon") presents the coming of judgment as in-process, or as imminently crashing down on them.

Some commentators believe this means that the rich that James addresses are irreversibly under God's wrath.[11] However, God's prophetic judgments in the OT were often conditional. As with

---

10 Hos 7:14; Amos 8:3; Zech 11:2; Isa 10:10; 13:6; 14:31; 15:2, 3; 16:7; 23:1, 6, 14; 24:11; 52:5; 65:14; Jer 2:23; 31:20, 31; Ezek 21:17. The one exception may be Isa 52:5, which is difficult to interpret.

11 E.g., Chris A. Vlachos, *James*, EGGNT (B&H Academic, 2013), 158–159; Peter H. Davids, *The Epistle of James: A Commentary on the Greek Text*, NIGTC (Eerdmans, 1982), 174–175; James Hardy Ropes, *A Critical and Exegetical Commentary on the Epistle of St. James*, ICC (T&T Clark, 1916), 282, although he

Nineveh, if the wicked would repent and turn to God, he might relent of the coming punishment. So also here, the rich could repent and perhaps avoid the coming miseries. But who exactly are "the rich," and are they believers or unbelievers? A conditional warning of God's impending judgment seems more appropriate for nonbelievers. Yet, the matter is not settled so easily since commentators are divided on whether the "rich" in James, especially in chapter 1, are believers or not.

In 1:9–10, James tells the "poor brother" (ὁ ἀδελφὸς ὁ ταπεινὸς) to boast in his exaltation and "the rich" (ὁ πλούσιος) to boast in his humiliation or humility (ταπείνωσις). Because of the parallelism with "poor brother," some commentators assume "the rich" are also brothers and thus believers.[12] But it is not grammatically necessary that the word "brother" be implied with "the rich" just because of the parallelism. Also, James says "the rich" will pass away in their humiliation and are compared to ephemeral flowers (1:10–11). Such a statement does not describe believers well. The command to "let the rich man glory in his humiliation" (NASB) should be taken as ironic: Let them boast for now, but their end is only eschatological humiliation "because they will pass away like a flower of the grass" (1:10). The causal phrase makes the most sense if the boasting is seen as negative, done by a nonbeliever who will be judged when he fades away. Such language would be extraordinarily harsh if the rich here were addressed as believers. But if "the rich" in verse 10 refers to nonbelievers, James does not necessarily condemn all wealthy persons as a class. As Joseph Mayor observed, the NT records wealthy righteous believers, and James's audience seems to have wealthy traders (4:13–16).[13] So then, James must be condemning a certain subset of rich persons.

---

suggests some might be Christians, but all are addressed as unbelievers under judgment.

12 So Moo, *James*, 36, 66–67. Mayor's commentary, published originally in 1892, lists a number of earlier commentators who interpreted 1:10 as "let the rich brother glory in his humiliation as a Christian," that is, glory in his identification with the lowly Christ and his people, not in his wealth.

13 Joseph B. Mayor, *The Epistle of St. James: The Greek Text with Introduction, Notes, Comments, and Further Studies in the Epistle of St. James* (1892; repr., Zondervan, 1954), 45, though Mayor does view the rich in v. 10 as believers.

As we will see from 2:5–7 and 5:1–6, that subset includes those who abuse and defraud the poor for the sake of their own comfort and honor.

The "rich" are more obviously nonbelievers later in the epistle. In 2:5–7, the rich are those who drag the poor into court and blaspheme the name of God. James mentions these rich men to emphasize his point that they should not honor rich men who come into their worship assemblies more than they honor the poor (2:1–4). And finally, in 5:1–6, the behavior is completely unbecoming of Christians, and the prophetic language used to denounce them is language reserved for those under God's wrath in the OT. Thus, in these two passages, the rich are presented as "wicked oppressors of the people of God."[14] I, therefore, agree with those commentators who view the "rich" throughout James as being nonbelievers who oppress the poor.[15] They are denounced not because of their wealth but because of their wicked use of social power that came with their wealth. However, as noted earlier, these nonbelievers do have the opportunity to repent of their wickedness and oppression and join the poor in their worship of the one true God. This conversion would necessarily be accompanied by a new way of viewing resources, namely, as a means to loving one's neighbor.

Having suggested that "the rich" in James 5:1 are nonbelievers under prophetic condemnation, we may continue examining the rest of 5:1–6. Verses 2–3 elaborate on the result of the rich's errant action of storing up treasure in the last days. He first says, "your wealth *is rotten* and your garments *are* moth-eaten" (v. 2). The Greek verbs translated in italics are in the Greek perfect tense-form (σέσηπεν, γέγονεν), which James probably uses to emphasize the state that results from rotting and being eaten by moths. We get a hint here of the real problem, that the stored-up treasure

---

14 Moo, *James*, 66.

15 Peter H. Davids, *A Theology of James, Peter, and Jude*, BTNT (Zondervan, 2014), 51 n. 69; Scot McKnight, *The Letter of James*, NICNT (Zondervan, 2011), 98–99; Luke T. Johnson, *The Letter of James: A New Translation with Introduction and Commentary*, AB (Yale University Press, 1995), 190–191; Ralph P. Martin, *James*, WBC (Word, 1988), 25–26; Dale Allison, *A Critical and Exegetical Commentary on the Epistle of James*, ICC (Bloomsbury, 2013), 205. Allison cites more than thirty other commentators who hold this position on p. 205 n. 73.

is completely static and useless, doing no good for the poor or for God. The adjective "moth-eaten" (σητόβρωτα) is used throughout the Septuagint as traditional imagery for something being destroyed.[16] The adjective also echoes Jesus's teaching to lay up treasures in heaven, where moth (σής) cannot destroy (Matt 6:19–20; Luke 12:33). The verb "is rotten" (σήπω) is used graphically in 1 Clement 25.3 to speak of the flesh of a phoenix decaying after its death. So, the result of storing up treasure in the last days is, first of all, that the accumulated wealth is static, rotten, and useless. These resources are not being employed for the good of the poor or for any of God's purposes.

Verse 3 adds the imagery of rust and corrosion. James says, "Your gold and silver are corroded, and their rust will be for a witness against you, and it [their rust] will eat your flesh like fire." Again, the perfect tense-form is used ("are corroded," κατίωται) to convey a resultant state of corrosion. James personifies this rusty wealth by depicting it as witnessing against the rich at the final judgment. He graphically and prophetically proclaims that the rust of their wealth will consume their flesh like fire.

Much evidence suggests that James is adapting his language from a specific Jewish tradition (Sir 12:10–11; 29:8–12), which similarly condemns the static hoarding of wealth. First, the verb "to corrode" (κατιόω) occurs in the Greek Bible only in Sirach 12:10–11 and James 5:3. Second, the noun "rust" (ἰός) is rare, occurring in only two other contexts in the Greek Bible: Jeremiah 1:10, 23; Ezekiel 24:6–12. The verbal form "to rust" (ἰόομαι) occurs only in Sirach 12:10; 29:10. Thus the rare word group (ἰός, ἰόομαι) occurs in only five contexts total in the Greek Bible, with three being James 5:3, Sirach 12:10, and Sirach 29:10. Third, like James 5, Sirach 12 and 29 teach about the use of wealth. Fourth, the terms "silver," "gold," and "treasure" all occur in James 5:2–3 and Sirach 29:10–11, in slightly different forms (Jas: ἄργυρος, χρυσὸς, and θησαυρίζω; Sir: ἀργύριον, χρυσίον, θὲς τὸν θησαυρόν). This linguistic and thematic evidence suggests James is drawing from Sirach's Jewish teaching on wealth, poverty, and resources. If true, then the idea that resources should be dynamic rather than static

---

16 Job 13:28; Isa 51:8; Prov 25:20; Sir 42:13; Isa 33:1; 50:9.

has precedence before James. Yet, while James draws from Sirach here, we will see that James promotes certain ideas from Sirach while omitting others.

Sirach 12 warns about not giving money or bread to the wicked; rather one should give it to the righteous, who will not harm them in return. One should not trust an enemy, because his wickedness corrodes like copper (12:10). Even if an enemy humbles himself, one should remain vigilant to guard against him. Sirach assumes that one should give alms and warns that one should give it to those who are righteous. Almsgiving was highly commended in ancient Jewish writings, sometimes even carrying the promise of salvation and forgiveness of sins.[17] According to Sirach 29:8–12, one should not make the humble wait for charity or turn them away. Rather, one should "lose silver for the sake of a brother and a friend, and do not let it rust (ἰόομαι) under the stone unto destruction" (29:10). The fact that the silver is "under the stone" shows that the person would be hiding it away for safekeeping, afraid to use it for positive purposes. Sirach's imagery might remind us of Jesus' parable of the servant who buried his master's talent in the ground out of fear. The master chided the servant for being wicked and slothful and for not at the very least investing it to earn some interest (Matt 25:14–30). Sirach continues again in this passage to emphasize almsgiving as the positive and righteous use of wealth. Rather than allowing it to rust under a stone, Sirach implores, "Dispose of your treasure according to the commandments of the Most High, and it will profit you more than gold. Store up charity in your treasuries, and it will deliver you from every affliction" (29:11–12).

While James agrees with Sirach that the rich who hoard their treasure and keep it static are wicked, he does not follow his lead by advising the rich to give alms to the poor as the way to merit salvation and thereby escape their condemnation. Given how

---

17 Tob 2:14; 4:10–11; 12; 8–10; Sir 3:30; 31:5. See especially among these Tob 4:10–11 (NRSV): "For almsgiving delivers from death and keeps you from going into the Darkness. Indeed, almsgiving, for all who practice it, is an excellent offering in the presence of the Most High." This subject is treated fully in Gary A. Anderson, *Charity: The Place of the Poor in the Biblical Tradition* (Yale University Press, 2014).

much James echoes Sirach's teaching from these two passages, the omission of almsgiving seems intentional. We might infer, first, that James wants to avoid the salvific connotations that almsgiving had acquired in some strands of Judaism. Second, we might infer that James does not view almsgiving as the sole inverse of hoarding static wealth. James would certainly follow Jesus by endorsing almsgiving (e.g., Matt 5:42; 10:42), but Jesus also recognized that almsgiving was insufficient as the sole positive use of resources, and could even be done hypocritically: "But give as alms those things that are within, and behold, everything is clean for you" (Luke 11:41).

For two reasons, James may also have in mind 1 Enoch 96:1–8. First, 1 Enoch 94–97 is a clear, extended passage of prophetic denunciation of the rich for their abuses of the poor. Second, 1 Enoch 96:4 says that if you misuse money, your heart will condemn you and "this very matter shall be a witness against you, as a record of your evil deeds."[18] This passage may have been part of James's inspiration for personifying the rust of the rich's wealth, which would condemn them at the judgment. In 1 Enoch 96:1–8, the author condemns the rich who "have water available to [them] all the time" and who "eat the best bread" and "drink wine in large bowls" (v. 5). But, like James 5, it does not condemn the rich simply for possessing wealth. Rather, they are denounced because they "carry out oppression, deceit, and blasphemy" (v. 7) and because they are powerful people "who coerce the righteous with [their] power" (v. 8). Love of money causes men to become greedy and oppressive so that they acquire goods to hoard. But neither 1 Enoch nor Sirach nor James condemns the possession of wealth in itself.[19] Rather, it is the unrighteous, static hoarding of wealth that is unjustly withheld from the poor laborers.

The rusted state of the rich's wealth in James 5 is the result of the main reason for their condemnation: they have stored up treasure in the last days. In the Jewish texts mentioned earlier, especially

---

18 Translation from James H. Charlesworth, ed., *The Old Testament Pseudepigrapha* (Hendrickson, 1983), 1:77.

19 Contrary to the claim of Allison (*James*, 204) that James views the wealthy negatively simply because of their wealth.

Tobit and Sirach, Jewish believers are encouraged to store up good works in heaven in their own personal treasury, which would grant them soteriological benefits in the judgment.[20] Jesus does not attach the same soteriological benefits to good works, but he similarly exhorts his followers to store up treasure in heaven through good works (Luke 12:21, 33; 18:22; Matt 6:19–20).

In contrast to Jewish admonitions to employ resources for the good of the poor, the rich that James addresses have stored up earthly treasures in order to hoard them for themselves. As Sirach says, they have stored their treasure under the stone, where it sits useless and becomes rusted and destroyed. James 5:4–6 elaborates on exactly how they have stored up these treasures. They have defrauded workers of their wages, keeping the money for themselves (5:4), which was consistently denounced throughout Jewish tradition.[21] The rich have also lived in luxury and self-indulgence (5:5). These expenditures do not mean the rich stopped hoarding wealth, but rather that they exchanged one form of hoarded wealth for another, namely, goods and luxuries. They have wasted their wealth on these indulgences in the "day of slaughter" (ἐν ἡμέρᾳ σφαγῆς), a phrase interpreted differently by commentators but that is best taken as a reference to the final day of judgment. The phrase has its background in the Hebrew traditions of God's judgment as a day of the slaughter of his enemies (e.g., Isa 30:33; 34:5–8; Jer 46:10).[22] James may draw the phrase directly from Jeremiah 12:3: "But you, Lord, know me; you have approved my heart before you; purify them for the day of their slaughter." 1 Enoch 94:9 refers to the "day of slaughter" as the day when God will judge the wicked rich. 1QH XV, 17–18 refers to the "Day of Massacre" as the eschatological day. So "the day of slaughter" here likely refers to the eschatological judgment of the wicked.

The result of their hoarding wealth in the last days is that they have "condemned to death the righteous." As in the OT, the poor

---

20 4 Ezra 7:76–77; 2 Bar. 14:12–13; 24:1; Tob 12:8–10.

21 Lev 19:13; Deut 24:14–15; Job 7:1–2; 24:10; 31:13, 38–40; Jer 22:13; Mal 3:5; Sir 7:20; 31:4; 34:21ff.; Tob 4:14; Matt 20:8; T. Job 12:4; Ps.-Phoc. 19. These references were taken from Davids, *James*, 177.

22 Davids, *James*, 178.

workers are here portrayed as having a "righteous" spiritual disposition presumably because they are unable to rely on themselves
for salvation or restitution. They must instead rely on God, and
many of them do; hence, the generalized characterization of the
poor as righteous. The final clause may cohere with this idea. It
can be translated either "he does not oppose you," referring to the
righteous man's inability to oppose the rich, or translated as "does
he not oppose you?" referring to God's opposition of the rich on
behalf of the poor. The latter option makes for a good prophetic
climax, fits James's polemical style, and also coheres with the near-
by use of the same verb (ἀντιτάσσω) in 4:6 with God as the subject
opposing the arrogant.[23]

The torturous treatment of the poor and the wicked use of
wealth are bad enough in themselves. Yet, when we consider these
evils in light of the meaning of *in the latter days* (Jas 5:3), we see
that their sin is even more egregiously intolerable. The first four
instances of the phrase "in the latter days" occur in the Pentateuch
(Gen 49:1; Num 24:14; Deut 4:30; 31:29). The other fifteen instances occur only in the prophets.[24] Genesis 49 prophesies that Ju-
dah will head up Israel and destroy their enemies, while Numbers
24 prophesies that a messianic king will fulfill this role (24:17–
19). But Deuteronomy emphasizes that, in the latter days, evil will
come upon Israel because they will fall away from God (31:29).
This evil includes exile, which for Israel lasted from the destruction of the first temple in 586 BC through the time of Jesus. Although Israel was restored from exile and the temple was rebuilt,
the glory of God never re-inhabited the temple, and thus, many
first-century Jews considered themselves still in exile until God's
presence would return to earth.[25] The latter days would be char-

23 Johnson, *James*, 305; William Varner, *James: A Commentary on the Greek Text* (Fontes Press, 2017), 349–351.

24 Isa 2:2; Jer 17:11; 23:20; 30:24; 48:47; 49:39; Ezek 38:8, 16; Dan 10:14; Hos 3:5; Amos 4:2; 8:10; Mic 4:1.

25 1QS VII, 5–7; 1QM I, 1–3; Tob 3:3–4; 14:5; 4Q504 III, 10-11; VI, 10–15; T. Benj. 10:11. First Baruch and the Epistle of Jeremiah are pseudepigraphs writ-
ten during the Second Temple period that are written (fictionally) to the Jews in exile after the destruction of the first temple. The letters likely intended to use the first exile as the basis for exhorting Jews in their day to live purely while in exile.

acterized by evil and tribulation, featuring especially false teachers and apostates.[26]

The early church understood themselves to be living in "the latter days," during which they were experiencing tribulation, false teachers, and apostasy.[27] They knew the latter days had begun because the Holy Spirit had come upon "all flesh" at Pentecost, which Joel prophesied would happen in the latter days (Joel 2:28–32; Acts 2:17). The fact that they were living in the latter days bears two implications for James's condemnation that the rich have stored up treasure. First, it is a time of tribulation, and the rich are thus taking part in the side of evil. They are oppressing the poor and mounting their sins for the coming judgment day. To whatever extent the poor workers were part of the church, the rich were persecuting the church by depriving them of resources necessary for life.

Second, consummation was imminent. Jesus' return is not like a steady walk toward earth with a known time of arrival but more like one waiting on the other side of a door, ready to appear at any moment in history. The imminence of Jesus' return creates an urgency about how we conduct ourselves and how we steward our resources. If history could consummate tomorrow, what point is there in hiding your riches under a rock to let it rust? Why defraud your workers when you cannot fathom how to spend all the resources you have anyway? We are reminded of Jesus' parable of the rich fool who hoarded up his grain for its own sake and whose life God took the next day to demonstrate the pointlessness of storing up treasures in such a way (Luke 12:13–21). So, in the last days, resources must be stewarded ethically, employed

---

Not all Jewish traditions held they were still in exile (e.g., Jud 4:2–3), but probably the majority did.

26 An end-time persecution is mentioned in Deut 4:30; 31:29; Ezek 38:14–16; Dan 7:21, 23, 25; 8:17–26; 11:28–12:13; 4Q169 frgs. 3–4, 2:2; frgs. 3–4, 3:3–5; CD-A I, 12–19; Sib. Or. 5:447–482; 4 Ezra 8:50; and elsewhere. False teaching is said to be part of this persecution in Dan 7:25; 8:25 and in other Second Temple Jewish sources. G. K. Beale, *A New Testament Biblical Theology: The Unfolding of the Old Testament in the New* (Baker Academic, 2011), 111, 124–26, 187–224.

27 Jas 1:18; 5:3; 5:7–9; 1 Pet 1:3, 20–21; 3:18–19, 21–22; 4:12–19; 2 Pet 1:16–17; 3:3; Jude 18.

for kingdom purposes with a sense of eschatological urgency, and not gathered under a rock only to rust away. And this last warning brings us to the final, positive point that James is making.

Resources Should Be Used Dynamically and Only as a Means

First, money must be used dynamically. The problem with storing up treasure is that it becomes static, rusted, and worthless. Considering the passages cited above from James and his influences (Jesus, Sirach, and probably 1 Enoch), we may conclude that resources are given by our creator to be employed with wisdom, integrity, purpose, and in ways that bear fruit. Some of the ways that resources can be used dynamically are mentioned in James, while others can be drawn from the rest of Scripture and from the modern fields of economics and development. For example, believers might bless others (particularly the poor) by giving gifts or alms (e.g., Jas 2:15–16); by creating jobs and paying workers according to the labor agreement (e.g., Jas 5:4); by investing so that resources would multiply and be employed in greater ways in the future (implied in Jas 5:2–3 and taught in Matt 25:14–30); by partnering financially with organizations that fight for legal and political justice on behalf of the poor (an implication of Jas 2:6); by saving wisely (not hoarding selfishly) to avoid future dependence (1 Thess 2:9), to support one's family (1 Tim 5:8), and to enable future service and generosity (1 Tim 6:18); by sponsoring community development efforts; etc. The principle at stake is that money must not be hoarded uselessly. It must be employed in meaningful, dynamic ways for God's purposes and especially for the sake of the needy, oppressed, and hopeless.

Another way of thinking about resources being used dynamically is to consider the theory of subjective value, which claims that an item's value is based on the utility it has for its owner. A resource has utility for an owner to the extent that it is able to achieve some end. Those who hoard excessive amounts of resources are achieving little to no end with their static resources. Hoarded resources thus have a diminishing return on utility, and so, each new unit added to the static stash has less value for the owner. But when those resources are transferred or exchanged for other resources that achieve some legitimate end, those resources increase in value. Through free and consensual gifts, services, and exchanges, even a limited amount of resources can increase in value if they have a higher utility for the new owners. This increase in value is the result of a dynamic use of resources.

One helpful reviewer of this essay commented that my phrase "dynamic use of resources" implies that I am arguing we must invest our resources into the expansion of production. Indeed, expanding production is one legitimate means of using resources dynamically. The explosive expansion of production starting with the industrial revolution has ushered in an unprecedented amount of wealth to the world and has helped billions escape poverty. Considering even the last four decades (1980–2019), the World Bank's data shows that the global extreme poverty rate has decreased from more than 40 percent to less than 10 percent. But at the same time, the expansion of the means of production is a macroeconomic issue. While Christians in democratic nations have a voice in their nation's economic policy, my phrase "dynamic use of resources" has the individual predominantly in mind because the individual is James's concern in his letter. So, as I listed examples of dynamic uses of resources, I only had in mind individuals or groups (such as churches) not governments.

Second, resources must be treated as a means and never as an end in themselves. The problem with the rich fool was that he was building a supply of crops simply for the sake of his supply. Similarly, the rich were defrauding workers because they treated money as an end. Thus, they treated their workers as a means, allowing them to cultivate the land that would produce plentiful crops for the landowners, while the landowners kept both the crops and the wages. James condemns the rich's treatment of the poor as a means to another end. Those who bear the image of God should never be used as a means to an end, just as God himself should not be. Resources should be the means by which we achieve our various ends, including the call to love our neighbor. The need to employ money as a means is intensified now as we live in the latter days when history could consummate at any moment and all static stores of treasure will witness against their owners on the day of judgment.

Conclusion

In James 5:1–6 we see a denunciation of rich landowners because of their misuse of resources and oppression of the poor. The presence of the latter days demands a more urgent and purposeful use of resources than self-centered indulgence. James, following the teaching of Jesus, warns that hoarding for one's own sake makes resources static and useless. Such hoarding will be judged by God. On the other hand, resources can be employed in a dynamic manner, not rotting under a stone but being used as a means in the economy for the benefit of one's neighbors, especially the poor. There are likely implications for a Christian view of modern political economy, since one might argue that certain economic systems better allow for the dynamic use of resources. One might also argue that certain systems encourage hoarding and greed, which would be the opposite of what James encourages. Also, one might note that James is a moral and prophetic voice to nonbelievers in his economic environment; might we be the same? In any case, the complexities of such an application from the first-century to our modern globalized political economy are too vast for this paper, and I offer the above suggestions as food for thought.

The definitive application we can take from James's epistle is that we must use the resources we have to love our neighbor, to treat others justly, and to resist hoarding resources for ourselves. There is a plethora of ways people can employ their resources today to achieve these goals, including but not limited to saving wisely, investing, spending, giving, employing, and creating. This essay has focused only on the principle of using resources dynamically, but the specific applications must be worked out with sound economic theory and with an appreciation for one's culture and political system. But in terms of the general principle at stake, no matter what our situation, we might ask ourselves each day, "Will my resources bear fruit for God's sake, especially for the poor?"

3

A Moral Case against the Universal Basic Income

David S. Kotter

Introduction

JESUS REPEATEDLY ADMONISHED his disciples to care for the poor, so the church needs to carefully examine the growing support for a new federal proposal to eliminate poverty: the universal basic income (often abbreviated UBI). Though the details differ, a UBI is a set of regular payments from the government large enough to provide a reasonable standard of living for every adult citizen. The intent of such regular payments would be to ensure that no individual was subjected to poverty.

An unexpected coalition of "Bootleggers and Baptists" has formed because some socialists see the UBI as a way to eliminate poverty and also many libertarian economists see direct payments as a more cost-efficient solution than the patchwork of federal programs currently in place.[1] If a UBI were implemented in the United States, one way to fund it would be by replacing all other welfare and need-based programs. In addition to such fiscal questions about the cost of such an initiative, the principal objection is that a UBI would eliminate the primary incentive to work and thus dramatically change the nature of society.

---

1 The expression "Bootleggers and Baptists" describes the coalition of proponents for abolition of alcohol in the United States from 1920 to 1933 and is based on the observation that regulations are supported both by groups that favor the ostensible purpose of a regulation as well as groups that benefit from undermining the same purpose. See Bruce Yandle, "Bootleggers and Baptists in the Theory of Regulation," in *Jerusalem Papers in Regulations & Governance* (Jerusalem Forum on Regulation & Governance, 2010), 1–15, http://regulation.huji. ac.il/papers/jp9.pdf.

This chapter will first provide economic definitions and background information on the UBI proposals currently under consideration. Second, the advantages and disadvantages of a UBI will be explored from the perspective of socialists, libertarian economists, and evangelical Christians. The third section will consider risks and opportunities associated with implementing a UBI at the national level and suggest that such a program may be inevitable. The final section will build a moral case against UBI and provide recommendations for evangelical Christians and local churches to emphasize the intrinsic value of work. Biblical teaching will be important because the instrumental need for work appears to be drawing to an end for the majority of people for the first time in the history of mankind.

Background of UBI

The discussion for a UBI is based on observation of three facts about poverty as shown below based on data for 2020:

1. The official poverty rate in the United States was 11.4 percent which represented about 37.2 million people out of a total population of 331 million people.[2]

2. The federal safety net was composed of 13 programs designed to alleviate poverty, and the total cost including Medicare in was $847 billion.[3]

---

2 Emily A. Shrider, Melissa Kollar, Frances Chen, and Jessica Semega, "Income and Poverty in the United States: 2020," United States Census Bureau, 14 September 2021, https://www.census.gov/library/publications/2021/demo/p60-273.html.

3 The 13 programs at the federal level include the Child Tax Credit and the Earned Income Tax Credit, Supplemental Nutrition Assistance Program (SNAP), Housing Assistance, Supplementary Security Income, Pell Grants, Temporary Assistance for Needy Families (TANF), Child Nutrition (school lunch), Head Start, Job-Training Programs, Women, Infants and Children (WIC), Child Care (block grants), Low Income Home Energy Assistance Program (LHEAP), and Lifeline (Obama phone). Robert S. Pfeiffer, "U.S. Welfare Programs: Antipoverty Programs," Federal Safety Net, accessed 26 November 2021, http://federalsafetynet.com/safetynetprograms.html.

3. The poverty threshold for an individual was $13,171, for a household of two was $16,733, and for a household of three was $20,591.[4]

Based on this data, if all the money spent on the federal safety net ($847 billion) were simply distributed equally to every poor person (37.2 million individuals), then each person would receive $22,769 which is 72 percent more than the poverty rate for a single individual ($13,171). Two poor married people would together receive $45,537 which combined is almost triple the poverty level for a two-person household. For this reason, less money could be spent on the federal safety net while still raising every single person out of poverty in the United States. These substantial savings would result from drastically reducing the high bureaucratic cost of employing people to administer the programs, test for people for eligibility, and build buildings and infrastructure for such transfer programs.

For this reason, socialists are in favor of the UBI to eliminate poverty for everyone. At the same time, libertarian economists admire the efficiency and savings associated with the UBI compared to the 13-program patchwork comprising the current federal safety net. Nevertheless, critics of the UBI argue that if the majority of people were provided enough money to live without working, then essentially everyone would leave the workforce. From this viewpoint, society would break down because most people would focus on eating pizza and drinking beer while leaving no one to do the work of making pizzas and brewing beer.

This controversy demonstrates that the UBI hinges on fundamental anthropological assumptions about human nature which have not and cannot be tested empirically in advance. Annie Lowery of the New York Times captured this uncertainty well:

> Poverty would disappear. Economists, needless to say, are sharply divided on what would reappear in its place—and

---

4 United States Census Bureau, "Poverty Thresholds," 8 October 2021, https://www.census.gov/data/tables/time-series/demo/income-poverty/historical-poverty-thresholds.html.

whether such a basic-income scheme might have some appeal for other, less socialist countries too.[5]

Further compounding this conundrum is the reality that UBI requires an "all or nothing" approach to implementation requiring careful consideration before pursuing such an approach to serve the poor. Unfortunately, preliminary studies have been unable to reliably predict the likely outcomes.

Christians should be in favor of both poverty elimination and the improved stewardship associated with a more efficient federal program. In addition, Christians are equipped with biblical information about anthropology that illuminates the hearts of people. The rest of this chapter will clarify the nomenclature of this UBI proposal in the next section then utilize biblical data to formulate recommendations for Christians and local churches afterwards. This analysis will be limited to the United States where current data is available and because the United States is likely to be the first country in history able to afford a UBI program aimed at completely eliminating poverty.

UBI Nomenclature

This section will explore the evolution of this proposal to eliminate poverty—from the early calls for a UBI for the poor, to Milton Friedman's practical idea of implementing a negative income tax. Considerable focus will be given to the UBI proposed by Charles Murray with further consideration of nuances brought by Michael Munger and other economists.

Thomas Paine, one of the nation's founding fathers and author of *Common Sense* in 1776, also penned *Agrarian Justice* which was an early proposal for a guaranteed minimum income.[6] Paine contended that the uncultivated earth was common property of

---

5 Annie Lowery, "Switzerland's Proposal to Pay People for Being Alive," *New York Times*, 12 November 2013, https://www.nytimes.com/2013/11/17/magazine/switzerlands-proposal-to-pay-people-for-being-alive.html.

6 A helpful summary and analysis of this work can be found in Andy Stern, *Raising the Floor: How a Universal Basic Income Can Renew Our Economy and Rebuild the American Dream* (Hachette Book Group, 2016), 172.

humans and that the property of people was limited to the value of the improvements. For this reason, he proposed a tax on ground-rent for every cultivated landowner so that the proceeds could be shared as a stake of £15 to everyone attaining the age of 21 and then a pension of £10 per year to everyone attaining 50 years.[7]

After the first world war, the philosopher and Nobel laureate Bertrand Russell proposed "that a certain small income sufficient for necessaries, should be secured to all, whether they work or not."[8] As part of his larger proposal for Guild Socialism, he considered this to be a guaranteed basic income for everyone and that a larger income should be given to those who are willing to engage in some work which the community recognized as useful.

Nobel laureate economist Milton Friedman advanced the practical implementation of this concept with a proposal for a "negative income tax" that would set a floor under the standard of living of every person in the country.[9] Friedman proposed (in 1962 dollars) that anyone earning more than $600 per year would be subject to a tax on all income above that level. On the other hand, anyone earning $100 below that level would receive a payment (i.e., a negative income tax) of 50 percent of that amount. Therefore every taxpayer, even those with no income whatsoever, would be guaranteed $300 per year for living expenses. Friedman argued that such a system would direct the efforts precisely at the problem of poverty, provide the most usable form of assistance in cash, efficiently replace other aspects of the federal safety net, and make explicit the costs borne by society. He also acknowledged that all such systems inevitably provided a disincentive to work because of the tax on earnings above the minimum and also the guaranteed income which would allow even able-bodied people to live without working.

In 2016, Charles Murray published *In Our Hands: A Plan to Replace the Welfare State* with a more refined proposal to eliminate poverty using UBI. His monograph will be the basis for the

---

7 Thomas Paine, *Agrarian Justice* (1797; repr., Stellar Classics, 2016).

8 Bertrand Russell, *Roads to Freedom: Socialism, Anarchism, and Syndicalism* (1918; repr., Routledge, 2013), 168.

9 Milton Friedman, *Capitalism and Freedom* (1962; repr., University of Chicago Press, 1982), 190–195.

analysis in the rest of this chapter.[10] In his work, Murray sought to minimize the disincentives to work inherent in the prior proposals, and in fact to seek positive incentives for individual behavior along with governmental savings and the elimination of poverty. Fundamentally, Murray proposed converting all welfare transfer payments to a single monthly cash payment of slightly more than $1,000 to every citizen aged 21 and older using a constitutional amendment. This would require each US citizen to file for a passport and to maintain a known bank account for the electronic transfer. The sole stipulation would be that everyone would need to pay about $3,000 per year for a catastrophic health insurance policy since Medicaid would be eliminated. Further, any additional personal income would be exempt from taxation up to $30,000 per year, and the government payment would be reduced by 10 percent for every dollar earned up to $60,000. Therefore, anyone earning $60,000 or more per year would receive a cash benefit of $6,500 from the government. This phased reduction schedule was intended to minimize disincentives to work.

Momentum for a policy consistent with Murray's proposal has been building among wealthy leaders of tech companies. Facebook founder Mark Zuckerberg advocated for the UBI during his 2017 commencement speech at Harvard.[11] Richard Branson, billionaire founder of the Virgin Group, wrote "A lot of exciting new innovations are going to be created, which will generate a lot of opportunities and a lot of wealth, but there is a real danger it could also reduce the amount of jobs. This will make experimenting with ideas like basic income even more important in the years to come."[12] Elon Musk, founder of Tesla and SpaceX, declared, "I think we will end up doing universal basic income. It's going to be necessary."[13]

10 Charles Murray, *In Our Hands: A Plan to Replace the Welfare State* (AEI, 2016).

11 Chris Weller, "Mark Zuckerberg Doubles Down on Universal Basic Income after a Trip to Alaska," *Business Insider*, 5 July 2017, https://www.business insider.com/mark-zuckerberg-universal-basic-income-alaska-2017-7.

12 Tom Murray, "Billionaire Richard Branson Thinks America Should Give Out Free Money to Fix Inequality," *Business Insider*, 3 July 2018, https://www.businessinsider.com/richard-branson-thinks-usa-should-give-out-free-cash-to-fix-inequality-2018-7.

13 Chris Weller, "Elon Musk Doubles Down on Universal Basic Income: 'It's

UBI Economic Analysis

This section will utilize the tools of economic analysis to describe the effect of the proposals to eliminate poverty. Such considerations were not necessary in the early centuries of the church because about 80 percent were subsistence farmers and the vast majority lived in abject poverty. With the thirty-fold increase in income around the world since the industrial revolution in the early nineteenth century, the church now needs to utilize such tools in making ethical decisions to truly address poverty alleviation. Though often statistically based and mathematically complex, the tools for economics are analogous to utilizing telescopes to see planets in greater detail or microscopes to better understand unicellular life. Notably, economists with integrity never claim to provide solutions, only to define trade-offs.[14] It falls to Christians to utilize biblically informed judgments to make conclusive policy proposals.

In the second quarter of 2021, total household wealth in the United States reached $142 trillion for the first time in history.[15] Given a population census of about 331 million people, this indicates that the wealth per capita in the United States was about $429,000. This means that if all the resources were somehow divided equally, every man, woman, and child in the United States would possess $429,000 in assets. Every family of three would be millionaires as a household, and this is an important indication that poverty could be eliminated in the United States in this generation.

In the same way, the gross domestic product in 2020 for the United States was $21 trillion, and this figure essentially represents the sum of the incomes of every person in the country. If this

Going to Be Necessary,'" *Business Insider*, 13 February 2017, https://www.busi nessinsider.com/elon-musk-universal-basic-income-2017-2.

14 For example, Thomas Sowell declared, "There are no solutions, only tradeoffs." Thomas Sowell, *The Vision of the Anointed* (Basic Books, 1995), 142.

15 Board of Governors of the Federal Reserve System, "Balance Sheet of Households and Nonprofit Organizations, 1952–2021," last modified 9 December 2021, https://www.federalreserve.gov/releases/z1/dataviz/z1/balance_sheet/chart/.

income were equally distributed among the 331 million people, then every man, woman, and child would have an income of over $63,400. The history of mankind has been characterized by famines and poverty such that a given country did not earn enough to support every citizen even if it were equally divided. This new phenomenon in the United States requires Christians to reconsider our ethical obligations to the poor.

Continuing with the same logic, the $847 billion that was spent in the United States in 2020 on the federal safety net programs and Medicare could in theory be divided among all the poor people to completely eliminate poverty. In fact, much less money would be required in supplemental payments because few people have precisely no income whatsoever. Estimates vary, but approximately $170 billion would be needed if the goal were to simply supplement income up to the poverty level.[16] Since the federal budget for 2020 was set at $4.79 trillion dollars, it would be more affordable to spend only 3.5 percent to supplement people up to the poverty level rather than the 18 percent of the budget spent on the 13 programs in the federal safety net.

As a side note, achieving such incomes would be a stupendous achievement in world history because US poverty thresholds are orders of magnitude higher than worldwide poverty standards set by the World Bank at $1.90 per person per day.[17] Almost all the people in poverty in the United States are above such a worldwide income level, and for those who are not, only $30 billion a year would be required to achieve that level.

Economic growth of individual income and personal wealth is moving forward exponentially, yet the amount of money to keep individuals out of poverty increases linearly with population. In other words, the number of calories needed to feed a person remains the same over time while real incomes (incomes adjusted for inflation) are increasing on average. Further, the cost of clothing and housing people is actually dropping in real terms, and so,

---

16   Robert S. Pfeiffer, "U.S. Poverty Gap," Federal Safety Net, accessed 27 November 2021, https://www.federalsafetynet.com/us-poverty-gap.html.

17   World Bank, "Global Poverty Line Update," 30 September 2015, https://www.worldbank.org/en/topic/poverty/brief/global-poverty-line-faq.

providing adequate clothing and shelter is easier than ever before in history. Given this new reality, the elimination of poverty in the United States appears to be increasingly affordable. Some would argue that a UBI to eliminate poverty is currently affordable in 2021, but even if it is not, a UBI undoubtedly will become more affordable with economic growth over the next two decades or so. The political will and other considerations are still lacking such that the UBI may not be implemented for decades, but the economic limitations for such a proposal are being overcome. For this reason, the ethical and moral objections to UBI need to be emphasized.

Given the prospect of eliminating poverty, the church needs to be conversant on the advantages and disadvantages of how such a program might be implemented, and both of these will be examined in the next section. However, as the economic limitations on UBI fall away, it is increasingly important to understand the moral case against such a proposal to alleviate poverty.

Advantages and Disadvantages of UBI

This section will review both the real advantages and enormous disadvantages of this poverty elimination proposal. In addition to these likely effects, any UBI proposal brings immense uncertainty of the impacts over time, especially with multiple generations.

First, the primary advantage of the UBI is the remarkable simplicity and efficiency for administration compared to the thirteen-program patchwork of the current federal safety net that addresses poverty. According to Murray's calculations on efficiency, poverty could be eliminated at a savings of hundreds of billions of dollars compared to the current system.[18] While still a proposal at the time of this writing, if President Biden's multi-trillion dollar "Build Back Better Framework" were to become law, then the savings from complexity reduction with a UBI would be even higher.[19]

---

18 Murray, *In Our Hands*, 102–104.

19 *The White House Briefing Room*, "President Biden Announces the Build Back Better Framework," 28 October 2021, https://www.whitehouse.gov/briefing-room/statements-releases/2021/10/28/president-biden-announces-the-build-back-better-framework.

Second, the UBI minimizes incentives for bad behavior and provides some incentives for good behavior. According to Murray's proposal, the initial $30,000 of income exempt from taxation ensures that poor people receive all the benefits of any work that they do. Ideally, people with more than $40,000 of annual income (i.e., a $30,000 salary plus the UBI) would be so invested in working that they would not be discouraged about the phaseout of benefits as their income rose to $60,000 per year. Further, being a "deadbeat" dad would be much more difficult as every man would have a known income from the government that could be garnished to support his children. The incentives for single motherhood would change since moms would bear the full cost of having a child on a fixed UBI income rather than receiving increasing benefits for each additional child according to the current welfare programs.

Third, a UBI would be a remarkably humanizing opportunity compared to the current fragmented system. Few non-poor people are aware of the cost of regulation to monitor and ensure that needy people are not illegally earning income or concealing savings and other assets. Jacob Levy captures underlying human costs often overlooked in programs of the current system:

> And so poor people will be subjected to another set of forms, another set of inspections, another set of surveillance and monitoring, another set of insults, another risk of false findings of guilt, for trivial financial savings.... And life for a sixth of the country's population gets worse, more unfree, more subject to the burdens and intrusions of micromanaging regulation.[20]

Alternatively, the UBI would lift people out of poverty with the easily verifiable requirements of being over 21, holding a valid US passport, and possessing a known bank account.

Fourth, the economic "voice" of the poor would be heard in the United States. Friedrich A. Hayek notes that the price system serves as a mechanism for communicating information of the needs of

---

20 Jacob T. Levy, "An Argument about Regulation," Bleeding Heart Libertarians, 4 February 2014, https://bleedingheartlibertarians.com/2014/02/an-argument-about-regulation.

economic actors all across the world.[21] Unfortunately, people with no money cannot send such price signals and the markets overwhelmingly reflect the desires of wealthier people. Further, charities donate not necessarily what poor people request but what they think poor people need. A UBI would resolve this discrepancy between the gifts of the wealthy and the desires of the poor.

Fifth, the unconditional nature of a UBI would reduce the distortions that are inherent in the current system of welfare which includes tests and limits of income and assets. In some sense, it would lessen the political pressure to continually raise the limits to advantage certain groups over others. Nevertheless, voter pressure to raise all levels would be intensified.

Finally, a UBI would release people from being defined by their jobs. Economist Michael Munger suggests that in the future people might respond to the question "What do you do?" with "spending time with my children" or "volunteering at the animal shelter."[22] Critics of Munger suggest the responses to the question might instead be, "Drink beer and play video games. How about you?" Elon Musk recognizes that this freedom presents the average person with a much more difficult question, "If there is no need for your labor, what is your meaning? Do you feel useless? That's a much harder problem to deal with."[23] This exchange highlights one of the disadvantages of the UBI, and several additional disadvantages will be examined in the remainder of this section.

First, a UBI in a democratic society unleashes unbelievably strong political forces. If people were able to vote for politicians who promised to directly raise the income of every voter, it is difficult to imagine any rational restraint on such a system. Providing all adults over 21 with $12,000 per year would cost $2.3 trillion dollars. While a partial guaranteed basic income or negative

21 Friedrich A. Hayek, "The Use of Knowledge in Society," *American Economic Review* 35, no. 4 (September 1945): 519–530, https://www.econlib.org/library/Essays/hykKnw.html?chapter_num=1#book-reader.

22 Munger claims, only partially ironically, that "jobs are overrated." Michael Munger and Russ Roberts, "Michael Munger on the Basic Income Guarantee," 16 January 2017, *EconTalk*, podcast, MPS audio, 1:04:17, http://www.econtalk.org/michael-munger-on-the-basic-income-guarantee.

23 Weller, "Elon Musk Double Down."

income tax would be less expensive, the pressure on the marginal cases to expand the program would be unbearably high. This internal pressure is relieved by the UBI since everyone enjoys the same benefits without any means of testing but at an extremely high cost.

Second, poverty is more than a monetary phenomenon. Giving money to everyone is too reductionistic of a solution to the multifaceted causes of poverty in the United States. Mental illness, drug use, poor economic choices, and sinful moral choices often combine to trap individuals in poverty. For example, nothing would not stop a person from purchasing a thousand $1 lottery tickets on the day the UBI check arrived and then starving for the rest of the month. Though the UBI is designed so that no one need starve in the streets, some extremely libertarian proponents seem to have little mercy for people who make poor life choices. Exchanging the federal government safety net for cash payments will stimulate private and church support but is unlikely to deliver on its promise to eliminate poverty. Further, providing everyone with a known income would provide a stimulus to those who would seek to exploit others.

Third, the complete implementation of a UBI also entails the elimination of all other programs which can help exceptionally needy people. On one hand, this requires much more planning and responsibility on the part of each individual. Churches and other civic organizations will need to step in and help those in extreme need who are not otherwise working for such benefits. A worse outcome would result from adding UBI while keeping all 13 programs in the federal safety net, and the political opposition would be tremendous against sunsetting any single program.

Fourth, a significant disadvantage of a UBI program is the need for an "all or nothing" launch even though empirical data on the outcomes are limited or nonexistent. For example, in 2017 Finland started an experiment to provide 2,000 citizens a guaranteed income independent of whether the recipients worked. Each randomly chosen participant received €560 (about $587) a month for two years.[24] Unfortunately, this sum of money is insufficient

---

24 Ivana Kottasova, "Finland Is Giving 2,000 Citizens a Guaranteed Income," *CNN Business*, 3 January 2017, https://money.cnn.com/2017/01/02/

to make a living and the two-year time limit on the trial does not accurately represent long-term behavior. The Alaska Permanent Fund, however, was started in 1976 to pay every citizen of Alaska a stipend from revenues stemming from the depletion of the state's natural resources. In 2018, the legislature of Alaska paid from the $55 billion fund an annual sum of $1,600 to every person in the state. Unfortunately, like Finland the amount was insufficient for a living, and also the rigors of living in Alaska suggest that this trial may not be generalizable to residents of other parts of the United States.

The point is that in experiments where people are guaranteed an income for two years, many treat this as a "sabbatical" time in life to pursue projects before returning to work later. On the other hand, given a lifetime of guaranteed income the question remains whether people would feel empowered to unleash creativity and entrepreneurialism in the workplace or would pursue a life of indolence and sloth. Further, the effects may not be helpful for children in the next generation who would grow up with parents who had never worked. In other words, implementing a UBI would necessarily be a leap into the unknown that might end up destroying the most productive economy in the history of the world.

Biblical Analysis of UBI and Recommendations for the Church

At the Jerusalem Council, the early church leaders encouraged Paul to remember the poor, something that Paul said was "the very thing I was eager to do" (Gal 2:10)[25]. In the same way, Christians of every age should be quick to imitate Jesus Christ and be eager to "proclaim good news to the poor" as a mark of true devotion to God (Luke 4:18; 7:22). For these reasons, this chapter need not elaborate on this point but rather recommend that any proposal purporting to eliminate poverty should receive the utmost consideration. In addition, Christians should be familiar with the tools of economics to evaluate soberly any program that requires such an

---

news/economy/finland-universal-basic-income/index.html.

25 Unless otherwise noted, all Scripture quotations come from the ESV.

"all or nothing" launch and has a universal impact on every citizen of the United States. In other words, Christians should use their heads along with their hearts to only support programs that truly will help others in need.

The foundation of this UBI proposal is the anthropological assumption that people will continue to choose to work when they no longer are required to work to pay the bills and earn a living. The Bible provides clear insight which has not yet explicitly appeared in the economic literature about the UBI: human beings are sinners who are created in the image of God. Sloth and laziness are to be expected from sinful people. The sluggard who despises work is aptly described in the book of Proverbs:

> The sluggard says, "There is a lion in the road! There is a lion in the streets!"
> As a door turns on its hinges, so does a sluggard on his bed.
> The sluggard buries his hand in the dish; it wears him out to bring it back to his mouth.
> The sluggard is wiser in his own eyes than seven men who can answer sensibly. (Prov 26:13–16)

In other words, the Bible affirms that sinful people will make up any outlandish excuse to avoid work, even that there is a lion in the road threatening to eat the potential worker. The Bible recognizes that instant gratification of turning over in bed often wins out over the strain of sweaty labor. Some people are like the sluggard who would have other people do everything even to the point of being hand fed by someone else. Finally, the overall problem of the sluggard is that he is wise in his own eyes and resists any sensible opportunities for change. As a result of this facet of sinful human nature, Paul admonished the Thessalonians to stay away from any believer who was walking in idleness and gave the unequivocal command, "If anyone is not willing to work, let him not eat" (2 Thess 3:6, 10–12).

Historically, hunger was the driver for most laborers. Proverbs 16:26 states, "The appetite of laborers works for them; their hunger drives them on" (NIV). In this case, it was the *instrumental* value of work (i.e., work was necessary to earn a living or even survive) that helped resist the temptation to be a lazy sluggard. Even apart from areas of the world under the influence of Christianity, the common wisdom has been that the *instrumental* value of work was the ultimate motivation.

On the other hand, the Bible is also quite clear that human beings are made in the image of God (Gen 1:26–28) who were created to work and designed to subdue creation. Under the direction of Moses and Bezalel the tabernacle of the Israelites was fashioned by "every craftsman in whose mind the Lord had put skill, everyone whose heart stirred him up to come and do the work" (Exod 36:2). Even slaves were admonished by Paul to consider a higher perspective of their daily labor when he told them, "Whatever you do, work heartily, as for the Lord and not for men" (Col 3:23). In this way, the Bible emphasizes the *intrinsic* value of work or that people were created to work in the image of God as co-creators subduing the earth. Some people along these lines people enjoy work and choose never to retire.

Indeed, Aristotle saw no intrinsic value to work compared to a life of contemplation and relegated the instrumental requirement of work to slave labor. If this Aristotelian viewpoint is more prevalent, people freed from the requirement to work might pursue more contemplative ventures or voluntarily serve others. Sloth may even prevail if people need no longer work in order to eat. From a biblical perspective, implementing a UBI would reveal whether people were primarily laboring for the instrumental value of work (i.e., "just to pay the bills") or because of the intrinsic value of work (i.e., "imitating the creative image of God").

Applying this important biblical insight to the topic of UBI, the program will fail disastrously if sinfulness prevails and if the citizens of the United States are primarily sluggards. If people are only working because of the instrumental value to pay the bills, then the UBI will leave no one left who is willing to work on third shift and other undesirable jobs. No incomes would mean no taxes would be available to sustain the UBI. Such a result would destroy the largest economy on earth and plunge hundreds of millions of people into poverty.

Alternatively, if most people understand and pursue the intrinsic value of work, whether because of personal desire or explicit obedience to God, then the UBI will be a force for tremendous good in the United States. People will be released to pursue volunteer work or riskier business ventures that likely will have greater benefits down the road.

Unfortunately, the population of the United States likely is divided between these two alternatives, and indeed every individual heart is divided between these two motivations. Professionals with fulfilling jobs probably will continue to earn higher salaries and find the $6,500 stipend of Murray's UBI proposal to be a very small disincentive to work. Laborers who are doing distasteful work on the third shift solely for a paycheck to make ends meet are much more likely to drop out of the labor force which would leave essential but unpleasant tasks undone. Such trade-offs will happen even within the jobs of most people which have at the same time fulfilling tasks and disagreeable chores. Employers will need to pay more to entice and induce employees to perform such unpleasant duties, to the point that a business model may no longer work. For example, if fast food cooks will only flip burgers for $40 per hour, then it may not be possible to supply hamburgers into the marketplace at a price that consumers are willing to pay. Indeed, even if burgers are still supplied, it is possible that price inflation will put such labor-intensive goods beyond the affordability of most customers.

Nevertheless, the church needs to come to grips with the possibility that a UBI is inevitable. At the current rate of 4 percent GDP growth, the United States economy will double in size to approximately $40 trillion a year over the next two decades. This staggering creation of wealth will make the UBI not only possible but probable. At the same time, the relentless automation of the most inhumane tasks and the gains in neural networks of artificial intelligence which devours even high-end jobs are both likely to continue relentlessly in the coming decades. This provides the hope that the *instrumental* jobs (needed only to pay the bills) will be eliminated and leave human beings to pursue work for its *intrinsic* value (as beings created to work in the image of God). Even so, work is commanded by God, "Six days you shall labor, and do all of your work" (Exod 20:9), leaving a day for rest. The church needs to recover and emphasize this biblical teaching on the intrinsic value of work.

In conclusion, the church needs to be active today in teaching about both the theology and economics of human flourishing. By introducing the category of sinful sloth, the Bible provides an essential contribution to this dialogue about a universal and extremely expensive UBI program. As the instrumental value of work declines over the coming decades, Christians will need to continue to serve one another in love whether at home, in the church, or in the marketplace (Gal 5:13).

4

The Alignment of Modern Economic Theory and Biblical Teaching

Robert L. Plummer

Introduction

DUTCH STATESMAN Abraham Kuyper famously said, "There is not a square inch in the whole domain of our human existence over which Christ, who is Sovereign over all, does not declare, 'Mine!'"[1] Even though virtually all evangelical pastors would agree with that statement, those same pastors are likely to neglect the field of economics as not relevant to their ministries. This is a serious error. In fact, economic principles are not only helpfully applicable to many aspects of daily life, but also modern economic theories overlap significantly with the teaching of Holy Scripture. In fact, economics is, in some sense, a form of modern wisdom literature.

Let us remind ourselves that "wisdom literature" was a varied genre in the ancient Near East. It consisted, for example, of monologues, as we find in Ecclesiastes, exploring the ultimate questions of meaning and life. Wisdom literature also took the form of dialogues or disputations, as we find in the book of Job. Such dialogues explore questions of life, death, suffering, good, and evil. Romantic poetry, like the Song of Songs, is also a form of wisdom literature—exploring and valuing the meaning of love in this broken world. And, finally, the form of wisdom literature most people first think of is Proverbs. A proverb is a succinct statement about the way life normally works. Biblical proverbs instruct us about

---

1 Quoted in Jay W. Richards, *Money, Greed, and God: Why Capitalism Is the Solution and Not the Problem* (HarperCollins, 2009), 7.

speech, relationships, friendship, marriage, money, and work—quite a bit, indeed, about money and work.

All languages and cultures have proverbs—wise advice in short, memorable expressions. Possibly due to the American fixation on productivity, many American proverbs deal with efficiency, money, employment, or contentment. For example, one common American proverb is: "A stitch, in time, saves nine." In other words, if you see a cloth beginning to tear and you stop to repair it now, it will prevent you from having to make a much larger repair job later. This proverb, while using the language of needlework, applies to any situation where a little forethought and intervention will prevent a larger clean-up later on (e.g., car maintenance, home repair, human relationship issues). Also, we recognize that a proverb is not a fail-proof promise. It describes the way things normally work. One might put a stitch in a shirt that is beginning to tear only to find out later that the tear has gotten worse. Poorly made fabric cannot be rescued by an early stitch. Even with such exceptions, however, this proverb is not false. It describes the way things *normally* work.[2]

Biblical proverbs are similar to this American proverb in that they usually have implied exceptions, but there is one major difference—biblical proverbs are inspired by God and, thus, inerrant Scripture. Biblical proverbs approve of what God approves and disapprove of what God disapproves. Such is not always the case with the modern economic "wisdom literature" we are going to survey. Such economic principles are not inspired, though they do often find parallel in Scripture. And perhaps, just as the Midianite Jethro came and gave Moses some practical advice about how to organize the overwhelming judicial demands he faced (Exod 18:1–27), even when economic principles do not explicitly parallel Scripture, we can still learn a great deal from them.

For the remainder of this essay, I'm going to overview seven principles from economics. After defining an economic principle, I will illustrate it from a popular children's story. Why am I doing this? (1) Using a children's story helps make the economic

---

2 This paragraph is adapted from my book *40 Questions about Interpreting the Bible*, 2nd ed. (Kregel, 2021), 254.

principles more understandable and memorable, and (2) I think it's fascinating how many American stories illustrate principles of industry and productivity. American children's literature is a hidden wealth of economic illustrations. The history of our nation is a story of amazing economic progress, and perhaps those values are subconsciously recorded and passed down even through the stories we tell our children. What I am saying here agrees with an article in *The Atlantic* entitled "Why the British Tell Better Children's Stories." The author of the article, Colleen Gillard, writes, "If British children gathered in the glow of the kitchen hearth to hear stories about magic swords and talking bears, American children sat at their mother's knee listening to talks larded with moral messages about a world where life was hard, obedience emphasized, and Christian morality valued."[3]

So, our continued procedure is this: I will discuss an economic principle. Second, I will illustrate it with a children's book. Third, I will point to possible parallels in Christian Scripture.

Principle #1: Comparative Advantage

The principle of comparative advantage means that individuals, companies, and even nations have specific comparative advantages in producing certain goods and services. One economics textbook says it this way:

> When people specialize [in the production of goods and services that they can provide at a low cost], they can then sell these products to others. Revenues received can be used to purchase items that would be costly to produce themselves. Through these exchanges, people who specialize in this way will produce a larger total quantity of goods and services than would otherwise be possible. Economists refer to this principle as the law of comparative advantage. This law applies to trade among individuals, businesses, regions, and nations.[4]

---

3 Colleen Gillard, "Why the British Tell Better Children's Stories," *The Atlantic*, 6 January 2016, https://www.theatlantic.com/entertainment/archive/2016/01/why-the-british-tell-better-childrens-stories/422859.

4 James P. Gwartney, Richard L. Stroup, Dwight R. Lee, Tawni H. Ferrarini,

What does this look like in real life? I like math, and I'm very detail-oriented when it comes to money. I opened my first bank account when I was six years old. When I was in 6th grade (age 11), I went to a summer camp. I remember the camp had stations where you could learn new skills. I enjoyed learning how to record checks in a register and balance a checkbook.

When I married my wife, she did not know how much money was in her checking account. So, we let that account sit dormant for a few months before we closed it. My wife is not good at personal finance, but she has other strengths. She is a gifted musician. She's a good decorator. She's good with colors. She likes moving furniture around, painting new colors on the walls, displaying new artwork, and the like. (I, on the other hand, left to myself, am content with mediocrity in the home decorating department.)

In our home, I have a comparative advantage in math and finance. I'm good at it, so I do it. My wife, on the other hand, has a comparative advantage in decorating. She's good at it. Our home works better when I focus on what I do best and she focuses on what she does best, within limits of course.

What's true on a personal level is true on an institutional level. The Southern Baptist Theological Seminary (where I teach) used to run an apartment complex. Why did the school decide to relinquish the management of its off-campus apartments to a real estate company? It gave up apartment management because the seminary's comparative advantage is in providing theological education. This activity is what Southern Seminary does well. Other people manage apartment complexes better.

Now, let's think about how comparative advantage applies to international trade. If you buy athletic shoes, they'll probably be made in China, Vietnam, or some other East Asian country. For the most part, the supply chain and labor costs in these countries allow for a comparative advantage in the low-cost production of footwear.

Let us turn to illustrate comparative advantage from a children's book: why does Santa use flying reindeer? As described in *The*

and Joseph Calhoun, *Common Sense Economics: What Everyone Should Know about Wealth and Prosperity*, 3rd. ed (St. Martin's, 2016), 16.

Cajun Night before Christmas, he could employ alligators.[5] But, if you look at the pictures of this delightful book, you will see that it's a lot easier to get down a chimney when you land on the roof than it is to to have alligators boosting you up the side of the house.

Do we find the economic principle of comparative advantage in the Bible? Yes, in many places. When Solomon needed a great amount of high-quality timber for the building of the temple (1 Kgs 5), he did not cultivate cedar trees in super-sized ancient greenhouses. Instead, he traded with King Hiram of Tyre to the North. Solomon traded wheat and olive oil (for which ancient Israel had the comparative advantage) for lumber (for which Tyre had the comparative advantage).

The principle of comparative advantage applies both in the physical and spiritual realm. From the apostle Paul's teaching in 1 Corinthians 12–14, we see there are different spiritual gifts in the church (different spiritual comparative advantages!), with the localized body of Christ functioning better when we exercise our gifts with diligence and humility—valuing and honoring the different gifts of those around us. In 1 Corinthians 12:17–18, Paul queries, "If the whole body were an eye, where would the sense of hearing be? If the whole body were an ear, where would the sense of smell be? But in fact God has placed the parts in the body, every one of them, just as he wanted them to be" (NIV).

Economic Principle #2: Signaling

Signaling is an economic term that refers to consuming goods and services with a primary purpose of signaling one's superior wealth. David Kotter observes "that Nobel laureate economist Michael Spence was the first to note that people spend resources to convey information about themselves to others and some activities are undertaken primarily as a signal to other people."[6]

An example of such signaling would be a Birkin bag. A Birkin

---

5 "Trosclair" (J. B. King Jr.), *Cajun Night before Christmas*, illus. James Rice, ed. Howard Jacobs, anniv. ed. (Pelican, 1992).

6 David Scott Kotter, "Working for the Glory of God: The Distinction between Greed and Self-Interest in the Life and Letters of the Apostle Paul" (PhD diss., The Southern Baptist Theological Seminary, 2015), 87. Kotter cites Michael

bag is a purse made by the French luxury goods company, Hermès. I typed "Birkin bag" in Google and found some used ones for sale, but none less than $20,000. A rather normal looking one on eBay was $89,950. Though it looked functional enough, it's main purpose is to show other people just how shockingly rich the owner is. That's signaling. Most of the readers of this chapter have never heard of Birkin bag, but the ladies who can afford them (or who can *almost* afford them) know what they are. Some women have more than one. I commend to you a podcast about the Birkin bag in the archives of *Planet Money*.[7]

Signaling, I think, is illustrated nicely in the children's classic *I Wish I Had Duck Feet*.[8] The child protagonist in this book is obsessed with having other kids admire him because he has something they do not. Now, to be fair, it is probably not technically signaling because he's not purchasing something that demonstrates his superiority. Rather, he fantasizes about having skills or accoutrements that other kids do not have.

Some portions of the book read as follows,

> If I had two duck feet,
> I could laugh at Big Bill Brown.
> I would say, "YOU don't have duck feet!
> These are all there are in town!"[9]

> I wish I had two deer horns.
> They would be a lot of fun.
> Then I could wear
> Ten hats up there!
> Big Bill can just wear one.[10]

Spence, "Job Market Signaling," *Quarterly Journal of Economics* 87, no. 3 (1973): 355–374, doi:10.2307/1882010.

7 Sindhu Gnanasambandan and Stacey Vanek Smith, "Episode 672: Bagging the Birkin," 10 November 2017, *Planet Money*, podcast, MP3 audio, 18:05, https://www.npr.org/sections/money/2017/11/10/563342363/episode-672-bagging-the-birkin.

8 Theo. LeSieg, *I Wish I Had Duck Feet*, illus. B. Tobey (Random House, 1965). Dr. Seuss wrote this book under the pen name "Theo. LeSieg."

9 LeSieg, *I Wish I Had Duck Feet*, 6.

10 LeSieg, *I Wish I Had Duck Feet*, 14.

I wish I had a long, long tail.
Someday I will, I hope.
And then I'll show
the kids in town
new ways to jump a rope![11]

Does the Bible recognize the concept of signaling? Absolutely! As Kotter rightly notes in his dissertation, we have Paul's admonition against signaling in 1 Timothy 2:9.[12] Paul writes, "Women should adorn themselves in respectable apparel, with modesty and self-control, not with braided hair and gold or pearls or costly attire" (ESV). Through this apostolic teaching, we recognize that a luxurious parading of one's wealth is a sin. We also observe that signaling is culturally and historically conditioned. There was a time when owning a mobile phone could have been considered a form of signaling. Now, many day laborers in developing countries own a mobile phone. Owning a mobile phone is no longer a form of economic signaling. If I were to go to Papua New Guinea and give an elderly lady a Birkin bag and she used it in a purely utilitarian fashion without any knowledge of its signaling value, there is no sin. Analogously, we recognize that in Paul's first-century context, pearls were considered extremely valuable, and from ancient mosaics and statues, we know that some ladies had elaborate hairstyles woven in gold to signal to their economic superiority. Nowadays, however, most pearl necklaces no longer have a signaling function and can be purchased quite inexpensively.

Economic Principles #3: Moral Hazard

According to an article in *The Economic Times*, "Moral hazard is a situation in which one party gets involved in a risky event knowing that it is protected against the risk and the other party will incur the cost."[13]

Why do teenagers get in more car accidents than adults? Of

---

11 LeSieg, *I Wish I Had Duck Feet*, 33.

12 Kotter, "Working for the Glory of God," 88.

13 *The Economic Times*, "Definition of 'Moral Hazard,'" accessed 14 January 2022, http://economictimes.indiatimes.com/definition/moral-hazard.

course, they're inexperienced and exploding with hormones, but there's also usually the problem of moral hazard. Mom and Dad will pay to fix the car—or the insurance will, and Mom and Dad pay for the insurance. Many teenage children have a perverse incentive to drive more dangerously. They enjoy all of the benefits of reckless driving and few or none of the possible economic risks.

Did you know that football used to be played without helmets? You might think that the lack of protective gear would have resulted in more head injuries. Actually, it didn't. People were more careful with their noggins because they didn't have the moral hazard of assuming that a helmet on their head removed the risk of injury. In an *EconTalk* podcast Greg Ip of *The Wall Street Journal* demonstrated how the introduction of helmets into the game of football created a moral hazard with an incentive to be more careless and actually resulted in more injuries.[14]

Why did the U.S. economy crash in 2008? One of the contributing factors was moral hazard. An article in Investopedia describes it this way:

> Before the financial crisis, financial institutions expected that regulating authorities would not allow them to fail due to the systemic risk that could spread to the rest of the economy. The institutions holding the loans that eventually contributed to the downfall were some of the largest and most important banks to businesses and consumers. There was the expectation that if a confluence of negative factors led to a crisis, the owners and management of the financial institution would receive special protection or support from the government. Otherwise known as moral hazard.
>
> There was the presumption that some banks were so vital to the economy, they were considered "too big to fail." Given this assumption, stakeholders in the financial institutions were faced with a set of outcomes where they would not likely bear the full costs of the risks they were taking at the time.[15]

---

14 Greg Ip and Russ Roberts, "Greg Ip on Foolproof," 11 January 2016, *EconTalk*, podcast, MP3 audio, 1:06:17, https://www.econtalk.org/greg-ip-on-foolproof.

15 Investopedia Team (rev. Robert C. Kelly), "How Did Moral Hazard

Arguably, when the Federal Reserve Bank of New York provided an emergency loan to Bear Stearns (a New York-based investment bank) in March 2008, it was creating an even more severe moral hazard that encouraged other financial firms to charge ahead with very risky investment strategies. These firms could assume they too would be rescued by the federal government. Some economists have argued that the government should have let Bear Sterns go bankrupt. The immediate pain would have been severe, but other financial institutions would have certainly pulled back on risk and been more cautious.

In the Dr. Seuss classic *The Cat in the Hat*, the mysterious feline visitor wrecks the house with impunity.[16] When mother comes back, indeed, he will no longer be there. The brother and sister will be left to answer to the wrath of their mother for the tsunami of destruction in their home. For the cat, it's all fun and no risk. Furthermore, in this situation of moral hazard, others are emboldened to enjoy the fleeting pleasures of destruction without having to answer to mom. Thing 1 and Thing 2 charge in with their own calamitous contributions. If the Cat is Bear Stearns, Thing 1 and Thing 2 are Lehman Brothers. Someone else will clean up the mess, so one might as well fly kites down the hall.

Does the Bible speak to moral hazard? In Proverbs 29:21 we read, "A servant pampered from youth will turn out to be insolent" (NIV). In other words, if you always rescue your servant from his failures, if he never has to bear the cost of them, he will grow up assuming you, as the master, will bear any consequences for the riskiness or wrongness of his behavior. He will end up being an insolent burden. Children, as well, who are not taught to bear the consequences for their ill behavior can be expected to behave disgracefully. Proverbs 29:15 says, "A rod and a reprimand impart wisdom, but a child left undisciplined disgraces its mother" (NIV).

Holding people appropriately accountable for their ill behavior can prevent others from going down that path. As Proverbs 21:11 says, "When a mocker is punished, the simple gain wisdom"

Contribute to the 2008 Financial Crisis?," Investopedia, last modified 29 October, 2021, http://www.investopedia.com/ask/answers/050515/how-did-moral-hazard-contribute-financial-crisis-2008.asp.

16 Dr. Seuss, *The Cat in The Hat* (1958; repr., Random House, 1986).

(NIV). Moral hazard can be avoided by making sure people bear responsibility for their own actions.

Economic Principle #4: Creative Destruction

According to the principle of creative destruction, as creative humans introduce new technologies, goods, and services, the prior inferior goods and services will eventually be surpassed and discarded. Though change is difficult, we should not mourn the loss of inferior goods. Indeed, it is this creative destruction that results in better products in a more prosperous world.

The term "creative destruction" was originally coined by the Austrian economist Joseph Schumpeter in his 1942 work *Capitalism, Socialism, and Democracy.* He defined the term as a "process of industrial mutation that incessantly revolutionizes the economic structure from within, incessantly destroying the old one, incessantly creating a new one."[17]

In one scene of the movie "Groundhog Day," the main character gets caught in a snowstorm and seeks out a payphone. I was struck by how odd this plot twist would seem to my children, who probably have never been more than ten feet away from a mobile phone for most of their lives. I was jogging a while back at a park near my home and took a photo of what used to be a payphone. It is now a gnarled slab of metal with some wires sticking out. As I took this photo, in my hand, I was holding a smartphone with immensely more functionality than a payphone. (And, there's no need to deposit 25 cents with each call!) With my Skype app, I can call anywhere in the world for free. I can listen to music, podcasts, audiobooks. I can learn Chinese with my language learning app. I can read my Greek New Testament and look up a word in a lexicon. I can check my email. The possibilities are almost limitless.

We must admit, however, that there is something lost with the end of payphones. How will my children really understand the

---

17 Carol M. Kopp (rev. Michael J. Boyle and Diane Costagliola), "What Is Creative Destruction?," Investopedia, last modified 23 June 2021, https://www. investopedia.com/terms/c/creativedestruction.asp.

movie *Groundhog Day*? What if they never get to call on a pay-phone themselves? Moreover, it is nice not to face the ever-present distraction of mobile phones. Perhaps it would have been better, when we saw this mobile phone technology emerging in the United States in the 1980s, to outlaw it. We could have let other countries take the lead in inventing things that destroy our way of life.

Creative destruction is a battle that has been fought and is being fought over and over. Why do French taxi drivers riot over Uber? Because through creative destruction a newer, cheaper, more efficient method of paid car service is emerging which threatens their livelihood.

Two centuries ago, French artisans who wove cloth by hand were angered by the mechanized looms and factories which were being built and threatened their traditional way of life. They threw their wooden shoes into the delicate factory machinery of the looms to destroy it. The names of those shoes were *sabots*. We remember those acts of defiance through the word we borrowed from the French—"sabo-tage."

In a *Wall Street Journal* op-ed, Daniel J. Arbess noted that one of the factors that will influence the future of the U.S. economy is the ability of the current working generation to adapt from American manufacturing and services to information technology.[18] Are we raising children who have an expectation to be learning new skills and who are not afraid to take risks to offer new goods, new services, start new businesses, start new churches and ministries? Are we raising an entrepreneurial generation? We no longer live in a world where a person can work for forty years for General Motors (or for a church, for that matter) and retire with a pension. Yet, have we moved beyond that loss to embrace the possibilities?

In the classic children's tale *Mike Mulligan and His Steam Shovel*, Mike Mulligan and his steam shovel, named Mary Anne, had had many years of successful digging, and as the story says, "Mike

---

18 Daniel J. Arbess, "The Young and the Economically Clueless," *Wall Street Journal*, 19 February, 2016, https://www.wsj.com/articles/the-young-and-the-economically-clueless-1455924699.

Mulligan always said that Mary Anne could dig as much in a day as a hundred men could dig in a week."[19]

Later, we read in the story, "Then along came the new gasoline shovels and the new electric shovels and the new Diesel motor shovels and took all the jobs away from the steam shovels. Mike Mulligan and Mary Anne were VERY SAD. All the other steam shovels were being sold for junk or left out in old gravel pits to rust and fall apart."[20] The wonderful twist to this story is that Mike gets one last chance to dig with Mary Anne. He and Mary Anne dig the cellar for the Popperville town hall, but unfortunately, once they have dug it, they find themselves stuck down in a deep hole without any way out. Wonder of wonders, in this economy of creative destruction (where steam shovels are being replaced by Diesel motors), Mary Anne's steam engine is able to be repurposed as the furnace for the town hall, which is built over her. Mike Mulligan also gets a new job as the town janitor.

Is there anything in the Bible about creative destruction? Before industrialization, globalization, and modern technology, the world did not face creative destruction with the same rapidity that we do today. And yet, we do find hints of the concept in the Bible. In the Old Testament, the Philistines, at one point, seem to have cornered the new technology of iron production—which is "creatively destroying" its predecessor of bronze implements. The Israelites are described as longing for this new technology, but their enemies are trying to keep it from them. We read in 1 Samuel 13:19–22,

> Not a blacksmith could be found in the whole land of Israel, because the Philistines had said, "Otherwise the Hebrews will make swords or spears!" So all Israel went down to the Philistines to have their plow points, mattocks, axes, and sickles sharpened. The price was two-thirds of a shekel for sharpening plow points and mattocks, and a third of a shekel for sharpening forks and axes and for repointing goads. So on the

---

19 Virginia Lee Burton, *Mike Mulligan and His Steam Shovel* (1939; repr., Houghton Mifflin, 1967), 1.

20 Burton, *Mike Mulligan and His Steam Shovel*, 14–16, capitalization original.

day of the battle not a soldier with Saul and Jonathan had a sword or spear in his hand; only Saul and his son Jonathan had them. (NIV)

Creative destruction, when looked at in light of the whole economy, has a positive impact, but on a personal level, it can lead to the loss of a job or industry—and to great economic uncertainty if one has put all of one's eggs in one economic basket, so to speak. The reality of economic uncertainty and ongoing change and the need to diversify and prepare for such uncertainty is found in the Bible. Though I readily admit, modern industrialization is certainly not in view. In Proverbs 27:24–27, we read,

> Riches do not endure forever, and a crown is not secure for all generations. When the hay is removed and new growth appears and the grass from the hills is gathered in, the lambs will provide you with clothing, and the goats with the price of a field. You will have plenty of goats' milk to feed your family and to nourish your female servants. (NIV)

We can paraphrase: "Have goats and be ready to milk them if your current success in a public service sector job falls through."

Economic Principle #5: The Importance of the Rule of Law and the Protection of Private Property

Why are some countries wealthier than others? Economists have repeatedly pointed out that two of the main correlating factors are the rule of law and the protection of private property. The rule of law means that the government acts in predictable and fair ways towards all its citizenry. Laws are not obscurely or randomly applied. There is a predictability to life because one does not have to fear some arbitrary or despotic action against oneself or one's business. Similarly, societies flourish when private citizens are able to obtain private property, borrow for or against that property, and live and invest with the confidence that their property will not be arbitrarily seized and that their property rights will be enforced.

The famed economist F. A. Hayek, in *The Road to Serfdom*, writes,

> Nothing distinguishes more clearly conditions in a free country from those in a country under arbitrary government than the observance in the former of the great principles known as the Rule of Law. Stripped of all technicalities, this means that government in all its actions is bound by rules fixed and announced beforehand—rules which will make it possible to foresee with fair certainty how the authority will use its coercive powers in given circumstances and to plan one's individual affairs on the basis of that knowledge.[21]

Jay Richards similarly reports,

> For decades, there has been a close correlation between the wealth of a country's citizens and the strength of that country's property laws. In general, the more a country (which includes the government and the citizens) protects private property, the more prosperous the citizens of that country will be.[22]

When there is a despotic government, which wrongly seizes people's property and arbitrarily mistreats them, human life does not flourish.

Apparently, these principles also apply to turtles. In Dr. Seuss's book *Yertle the Turtle*, Yertle arrogates to himself the right to arbitrarily boss others around and seize their freedom by forcing them to stand on each other's backs, with Yertle finally on the top.[23] Essentially, Yertle is a dictator who seizes from his subjects their freedom and thereby squashes their creative economic potential. In one page of the book, we see Mac at the bottom of the turtle pile, where he observes, "I know up there on top, you are seeing great sights, but down here at the bottom we too should have our rights."

---

21 F. A. Hayek, *The Road to Serfdom: Text and Documents: The Definitive Edition*, vol. 2 of *The Collected Works of F. A. Hayek*, ed. Bruce Caldwell (1944; repr., The University of Chicago Press, 2007), 112.

22 Richards, *Money, Greed, and God*, 95.

23 Dr. Seuss, *Yertle the Turtle and Other Stories* (Random House, 1958).

Rights to private property and fair treatment under the law cause both turtle and human societies to flourish.

In the Ten Commandments, we read, "Thou shalt not steal" (Exod 20:15 KJV). A command not to steal assumes the right to private property, a right supported by many other regulations about stealing, punishment, and restitution throughout the Bible. Similarly, the authors of Scripture are consistently concerned with equity, fairness, and justice. Repeated warnings are given throughout the Old Testament, that in settling judicial disputes, favoritism should not be shown either to the rich or to the poor (Lev 19:15; Jer 22:16; Ezek 22:29). Neither crony capitalism nor liberation theology cause human life to flourish.

Economic Principle #6: The Law of Unintended Consequences

Economists point out that by changing even small things in our lives, churches, institutions, or governments, we often create a cascade of other effects and incentives we did not anticipate. In his classic book *Economics in One Lesson*, Henry Hazlitt writes, "The art of economics consists in looking not merely at the immediate but at the longer effects of any act or policy; it consists in tracing the consequences of that policy not merely for one group but for all groups."[24] Similarly, economists Gwartney and his co-authors write, "Too often the long-term consequences, or the secondary effects, of an action are ignored."[25]

There are countless examples of this principle. One of the most frequently cited examples is rent control. Gwartney and others point out that when the government artificially forces landlords to take lower than market-value rent for an apartment, there are all kinds of pernicious effects:

1. Investors build less housing where it is needed most (because they anticipate a low or arbitrarily adjusted rate of return)

---

24 Henry Hazlitt, *Economics in One Lesson: The Shortest & Surest Way to Understand Basic Economics* (Three Rivers Press, 1962, 1979), 17.

25 Gwartney et al., *Common Sense Economics*, 40.

2. Owners of current housing fail to maintain it well because of slim profits.

3. Residents forego employment and other opportunities that would relocate them because rent control has perversely incentivized them to be immobile.

I have no doubt that people enacting rent controls are genuinely trying to deal with the issue of affordable housing, but the unintended consequences prevent market forces from dealing with issues of shortage. Swedish economist Assar Lindbeck famously said, "In many cases rent control appears to be the most efficient technique presently known to destroy a city, except for bombing."[26]

In the modern classic *If You Give a Mouse a Cookie*, the young protagonist discovers, "If you give a mouse a cookie, he's going to want a glass of milk, and when you give him a glass of milk, he'll want a straw, and when he's finished he'll ask for a napkin,"[27] and so on and so on and so on, until the mouse is overfed and over-entertained and the boy is exhausted. For society and mice to flourish, we need to think carefully about the far-reaching effects of our economic policies on the personal, institutional, and societal levels.

Does the Bible speak to unintended consequences? Proverbs reports that actions we take today can have long-term consequences for us and our children. Proverbs 6:10–11 warns, "A little sleep, a little slumber, a little folding of the hands to rest and poverty will come on you like a thief and scarcity like an armed man" (NIV). To bring this example into modern times, there's nothing wrong with spending a little extra time every day checking the news or taking in the social media feed on your phone, is there? Until one discovers that "a little time" has become 4–6 hours per day, and one's work, ministry, family, and personal life have suffered.

26 This quote is found in James P. Gwartney, Richard L. Stroup, and Dwight R. Lee, *Common Sense Economics: What Everyone Should Know about Wealth and Prosperity*, 2nd. ed (St. Martin's, 2005), 37.

27 Laura Numeroff, *If You Give a Mouse a Cookie*, illus. Felicia Bond (Harper Collins, 1985).

Economic Principle #7: Monetary Policy

It is a very strange reality to live with a fiat currency. The ten-dollar bill in your wallet or purse is worth $10 solely because our federal government has printed the number 10 on there and said it is so. How the Federal government manages this supply of money through printing, distribution, interest rates, policies with banks and bonds, is known as monetary policy.

The glossary in one economics text defines monetary policy as "the deliberate control of the national money supply and, in some cases, credit conditions, by the government. This policy establishes the environment for market exchange."[28] One of the main goals of monetary policy is to maintain a stable value to the currency, with only slight and predictable inflation. Thus, for example, you'd like to know that your $10 this year will still buy two Happy Meals at McDonalds—or possibly almost buy the two meals with maybe another 20 cents or so thrown in. What if, however, next year, two Happy Meals cost $40 or $200? What would saving, investing, and buying look like in that world of hyperinflation? Google "Venezuela economy" and read a couple of news articles and you will see what that looks like.

Our own country is endangering the long-term stability of our currency through the massive national debt and unsustainable levels of social programs. If there's nothing else of benefit in your reading of this chapter, certainly it was worth your time to find out about this final children's book *Roxaboxen*.[29] In this delightful book, the children of a neighborhood in the arid Western United States create a play society on a hill near them. Because of all the abandoned wooden boxes there, they name it "Roxaboxen." There are all kinds of items for sale or trade in Roxaboxen—wood boxes, big rocks, flowers, sticks, abandoned bottles. And, in the pretend world of children, there is also pretend ice cream to buy, horses to acquire, and fees to get out of jail.

What is the currency in Roxaboxen? Hear these words from the book:

---

28 Gwartney et al., *Common Sense Economics*, 3rd. ed., 243.

29 Alice McLerran, *Roxaboxen*, illus. Barbara Cooney (HarperCollins, 1991).

When Marian dug up a tin box filled with round black pebbles everyone knew what it was: it was buried treasure. Those pebbles were the money of Roxaboxen. You could still find others like them if you looked hard enough. So some days became treasure-hunting days, with everybody trying to find that special kind. And then on other days you might just find one without even looking.[30]

So, in Roxaboxen, we have a very stable supply of money, with only slight increases possible—and that achieved by hard work—such that prices remained stable. No hyperinflation.

In *Common Sense Economics*, Gwartney and his co-authors note, "A stable monetary policy is essential for the control of inflation, efficient allocation of investments, and achievement of economic stability."[31] A desire for a stable store of value is, of course, the attraction of digital currencies like Bitcoin, but at this stage, it's an extremely volatile and speculative store of value. In Bible times, people used gold, silver, and copper for currency. It is true, however, that sometimes someone would try to cheat others—perhaps by saying they were giving someone five-shekel weight of silver, but the scale was flawed. It was only four-and-a-half-shekel weight of silver. In Proverbs 11:1, we read, "The LORD detests dishonest scales, but accurate weights find favor with him" (NIV).

We live in a very different day with a fiat currency, but it seems that what is wrong for the individual (to dilute the value of the currency and thus harm the recipient) should also be wrong on a governmental scale. I admit, though, that this currency devaluation is (arguably) not played out at the same level of conscious dishonesty.

Conclusion

One of the main purposes of this chapter is to invite you, the reader, to discover the modern "wisdom literature" of economics and to see that principles of modern economics are often paralleled in

---

30 McLerran, *Roxaboxen*, 6.

31 Gwartney et al., *Common Sense Economics*, 3rd. ed., 78.

the Bible. I hope this chapter has whetted your appetite for further economic reflection and study. For "next steps," I recommend you (1) explore the many free resources and links at thefaithandwork-project.com (2) subscribe to the *Planet Money* podcast, and (3) read *Common Sense Economics*.

5

Almsgiving in the Evangelical Tradition

Joseph C. Harrod

Introduction

ELSEWHERE, I HAVE ARGUED for considering the biblical practice of almsgiving as a normative spiritual discipline.[1] The gist of that argument was that care for the poor was part of the vital religion of Israel in the Old Testament and continued to characterize the early church in the New Testament and beyond. Almsgiving is "intentional, tangible relief given to alleviate the suffering of the poor."[2] One part of that original article considered the place of almsgiving as a discipline among early evangelicals and this present article expands that survey. Care for the poor has always been a hallmark of evangelical activism.[3] This article surveys several early evangelical reflections on almsgiving that connect the practice to the formation of godliness. Many early evangelicals considered almsgiving as important for the formation of a truly Christian spirituality.

Evangelicalism emerged within Protestantism during the first third of the eighteenth century as a trans-Atlantic movement that emphasized the authority of Scripture, the centrality of the cross, the necessity of conversion, the necessity of active engagement,

---

1 Joseph C. Harrod, "The Neglected Discipline of Almsgiving," in *Journal of Spiritual Formation and Soul Care* 12, no. 1 (2019): 89–111.

2 Harrod, "Neglected Discipline of Almsgiving," 90.

3 David Bebbington, following the work of Heasman, notes that up to three-quarters of organized charities in Great Britain from 1850–1900 had direct or significant evangelical control. See David Bebbington, *Evangelicalism in Modern Britain: A History from the 1730s to the 1980s* (Routledge, 1989), 120.

and the inward ministry of Holy Spirit.[4] The movement has always been trans-denominational and rapidly spread from its Anglophone roots globally, especially during the nineteenth and twentieth centuries. This article's focus is on *early* evangelicals in England and New England, whose ministries flourished during the Great Awakening of the mid-eighteenth century and subsequent revivals of religion that followed. It considers the movement's influential leaders like John Wesley and Jonathan Edwards as well as those with more localized influence like Samuel Davies and Andrew Fuller. I have also sought to include women from New and Old England like Sarah Osborn and Mary Lyth to show that the spiritual importance of care for the poor was not restricted to the movement's leaders alone but was shared by ordinary and faithful church members.

Almsgiving and Spiritual Life

For evangelicals, true religion began inwardly by a supernatural work of the Holy Spirit, and it was the Spirit's continued presence that animated and directed a person's practices (or "religious duties") such that these activities were not merely expressions of self-love or of a person's natural bent, but genuine acts of devotion. A challenge for preachers was that those in their congregations might perform religious activities like fasting, praying, or caring for the poor for disordered or selfish reasons. Early evangelicals made sure to point out the difference between these two motives. More positively, the act of almsgiving offered a tangible way to deal with certain sins.

---

4 This definition follows a slightly modified version of David Bebbington's now classic statement in *Evangelicalism in Modern Britain*, 2–3. In including Pneumatology as a defining hallmark of evangelicalism, I am relying on my own research in the primary texts and also following the lead of Michael A. G. Haykin and Kenneth J. Stewart, eds., *The Advent of Evangelicalism: Exploring Historical Continuities* (B&H Academic, 2008) as well as Thomas Kidd, *The Great Awakening: The Roots of Evangelical Christianity in Colonial America* (Yale University Press, 2007). This approach differs from the very fine treatment of evangelical piety by Tom Schwanda, *The Emergence of Evangelical Spirituality: The Age of Edwards, Newton, and Whitefield* (Paulist, 2016), 1–2. Schwanda follows Bebbington's quadrilateral but acknowledges scholarly disagreement over the definition.

Virginia Presbyterian Samuel Davies (1723–1761) sought to help hearers distinguish "evangelical holiness" from mere "morality," when he observed that "a generous temper may incline to give alms; for the Lord's sake is omitted."[5] Evangelicals warned against the sin of selfishness. The Massachusetts pastor-theologian Jonathan Edwards (1703–1758) provided a deep analysis of the sin of self-love as part of a sermon series from 1 Corinthians 13, preached in the late 1730s.[6] Samuel Hopkins (1721–1803), abolitionist theologian and Congregationalist pastor in Newport, Rhode Island, expanded Edwards's emphasis when he offered nuanced reflections on the relationship between one's motives for benevolence and personal holiness.[7]

Caring for the poor offered an opportunity to acknowledge God's kindness towards his creatures through resisting the sin of ingratitude. Samuel Davies urged Christians to cultivate such gratitude towards God through their care for the poor: "Therefore let God be acknowledged the supreme, the original Benefactor of the world, and the proper Author of all our blessings; and let his creatures, in the height of their benevolence and usefulness, own that they are but the distributors of his alms, or the instruments of conveying the gifts of his hand."[8]

Some early evangelicals warned their audiences that almsgiving, and other religious duties, could be risky if their performance brought a false sense of security. Thomas Adam (1701–1784), Anglican rector in Lincolnshire, noted that even though Cornelius was a pious man known to care for the poor (Acts 10), his benevolence could not save him, for he still needed salvation through the

---

5 Samuel Davies, "Sermon 49: The Divine Life in the Souls of Men Considered," in *Sermons on Important Subjects*, vol. 2, 4th ed. (Robert Carter, 1845), 394, 397.

6 See Jonathan Edwards, "Charity Contrary to a Selfish Spirit," in *WJE*, vol. 8, *Ethical Writings*, ed. Paul Ramsey (Yale University Press, 1989), 253–272. The series was "Charity and Its Fruits," preached in 1738.

7 Samuel Hopkins, *An Inquiry into the Nature of True Holiness* (William Durell, 1791), chap. 4 (esp. pp. 66–70 and 88–91).

8 Samuel Davies, "Sermon 25: Ingratitude to God an Heinous But General Iniquity," in *Sermons on Important Subjects*, vol. 1, 4th ed. (Robert Carter, 1845), 470.

blood of Jesus and the inward ministry of the Spirit.[9] Evangelical ministers reminded their congregations that they needed to experience the presence of Christ; not merely to hear *about* him but to hear *him*. Baptist minister Benjamin Beddome (1717–1795) suggested that people sometimes used spiritual practices like almsgiving to dampen Christ's patient calling: "Sometimes they think to shake off their convictions by rushing into the cares or pleasures of the world. Sometimes they attempt to drown Christ's knockings by their prayers, humiliations, almsgivings, and other religious duties."[10]

Evangelicals also recognized almsgiving as a formative practice. John Guyse (1680–1761), English Independent minister, saw almsgiving as a practical way for believers to curb covetousness and to imitate the generosity of the Father and the Son.[11] Guyse preached from Proverbs 11:24, "There is that scattereth, and yet increaseth; and there is that witholdeth more than is meet, but it tendeth to poverty." Believing that this, and related Proverbs, formed the foundation of New Testament care for the poor, Guyse explained that the second person in this Proverb, the one who "withholds more than is necessary," exhibits the sin of covetousness.[12] The Proverb presents a paradox: by hoarding his money, this person actually experiences poverty in his soul. By contrast, the one who exercises care for the poor takes on the generosity of the Father and the care of the Son. Since care for the poor was enjoined under the Law, the one who exercises such care experiences the "inexpressible pleasure" consistent with obedience.[13]

Hannah More (1745–1833), playwright, philanthropist, and educator reflected on spiritual practices in *Practical Piety* (1812), noting the interplay between outward actions and inward devotion.[14] More considered the structure of Jesus's Sermon on the

---

9 Thomas Adam, *Evangelical Sermons* (London, 1781), 114.

10 Benjamin Beddome, *Twenty Short Discourses Adapted to Village Worship or the Devotions of the Family*, vol. 1, 2nd ed. (J. W. Morris, 1807), 39.

11 John Guyse, *A Collection of Seventeen Practical Sermons on Various and Important Subjects* (Edward Dilly, 1756), 208–211.

12 Guyse, *Seventeen Practical Sermons*, 208.

13 Guyse, *Seventeen Practical Sermons*, 210.

14 Hannah More, *Practical Piety: or, the Influence of the Religion of the Heart*

Mount important, noting that Jesus instructed his followers on holiness, love, and almsgiving *before* offering his model prayer. Here, care for the poor was one "habitual tendency" that believers undertake to keep their hearts ready for prayer: "Let us learn from this that the preparation of prayer is therefore to live in all those pursuits which we may safely beg of God to bless, and in a conflict with all those temptations into which we pray not to be led."[15]

Evangelical concern for the relief of the poor also extended to those who were themselves impoverished. Sarah Osborn (1714–1796) of Newport, Rhode Island, chronicled her quite ordinary life in an extraordinary memoir and decades' worth of diaries.[16] Married as a teenager, Sarah was widowed before the age of twenty, and nine years later suffered financial ruin through her second husband's bankruptcy. She started a boarding school in her home as a way to earn money and was the regular recipient of charity. Nevertheless, Sarah believed caring for those who were poorer than her was a Christian responsibility that she took seriously. In November 1751, Sarah worried aloud in her diary about how she might find money to give for a thanksgiving collection for the poor. The next day, however, she recorded that she had found a way to participate, but even more importantly, she had found numerous reasons to be thankful for God's providential care for her in the midst of her poverty.[17] Sarah's expressed thankfulness opens a window into her spirituality.

Sarah Osborn believed that God had made her poor in order to curb her selfishness and covetousness.[18] She prayed that God would supply her family's needs but also that he would help her remember the "poor and needy, the fatherless and widow, the

---

on the Conduct of the Life (Richard Scott, 1812).

15 More, *Practical Piety*, 64.

16 For a modern analysis of Osborne, see Catherine A. Brekus, *Sarah Osborn's World: The Rise of Evangelical Christianity in Early America* (Yale University Press, 2013).

17 Sarah Osborn, *Memoirs of the Life of Mrs. Sarah Osborn, who Died at Newport, Rhode Island, on the Second Day of August, 1796, In the Eighty Third Year of Her Age* (Leonard Worcester, 1799), 109.

18 Osborn, *Memoirs*, 55. Sarah's pastor, Samuel Hopkins, added an editorial footnote commending her theology and example at this point.

afflicted and tempted soul."[19] In the midst of winter 1761, Sarah prayed that God would work through those who had the means to provide for the poor and blessed him on account of those whom he had moved to care for her and her family.[20] By that November, Sarah was again thinking of thanksgiving collections and her desire to contribute collided with her own poverty:

> Now let me prepare, as God allows me, free will and thank offerings, to refresh his ministers, and relieve his poor. O that self may be entirely laid aside; and with a single eye to the glory of God, O may I cast in the mites he allows me, be it more or less, with cheerfulness and delight. Dearest Lord, I cannot be profitable to thee. But as I am, through boundless grace, thine own, use me in thy service for the good of others.[21]

Andrew Fuller (1754–1815), British Baptist theologian and missionary advocate of the late eighteenth century, saw care for the poor as a hallmark of genuine piety. Commenting upon Matthew 5:7, "Blessed are the merciful," Fuller warned Christians: "Whatever pretences we may make to orthodoxy, or to devotion, if we show no mercy to the poor and the afflicted, we shall on a future day meet with judgement without mercy."[22] Reflecting on Matthew 6:1–8, Fuller noted that the disciples to whom the Sermon on the Mount was first addressed were working-class men who practiced self-denial in meeting the needs of the poor. He lamented that such care seemed unusual in his day despite the Scriptural call, for "true religion always teaches men to be merciful."[23] In light of

---

19 Osborn, *Memoirs*, 211.

20 Osborn, *Memoirs*, 262.

21 Osborn, *Memoirs*, 280.

22 Andrew Fuller, "On the Beatitudes, Matthew 5.1–12," in *WAF*, vol. 8 (S. Converse, 1825), 192. I retain Fuller's spelling here.

23 Andrew Fuller, "On Alms-giving and Prayer, Mat. 6.1–8," in *WAF*, 8:213. Fuller found Jesus's admonition to give secretly necessary because of the heart's proclivity to corruption. Were it not for Jesus's training to practice one's almsgiving before God's eyes alone, many would be inclined to give only for public recognition, yet the heart of some was so deceitful that "secrecy itself may become a cloak for avarice" (8:213–214).

these warnings against selfishness and encouragements to generosity, several particular evangelical reflections bear mention.

John Wesley

Among early evangelicals, John Wesley's (1703–1791) concern for the poor is well documented and certainly influenced later emphases on the poor among Wesleyan-rooted movements such as the Free Methodists, Salvation Army, and the Church of the Nazarene.[24] Wesley's heritage was High-Church Anglican, the chosen religion of his parents Samuel and Susannah, but the impact of German Pietism vis-à-vis the Moravians and Wesley's own reading of authors like Philipp Jacob Spender (d. 1705) is well attested.

Wesley considered almsgiving an act of *mercy* as distinguished from acts of *piety*.[25] For Wesley, acts of piety included prayer, searching the Scriptures, receiving the Lord's Supper, fasting, and Christian conference, and such acts of piety were commonly labeled "means of grace."[26] Such acts of piety were, for Wesley, hallmarks of the pure New Testament church as described in Acts 2 and were Christ-ordained means "for conveying his grace to the souls of men," thus forming them in holiness.[27] In one significant sermon, John Wesley indicated that

---

24 For a helpful summary of this later influence, see Donald W. Dayton, "'Good News to the Poor': The Methodist Experience after Wesley," in *The Portion of the Poor: Good News to the Poor in the Wesleyan Tradition*, ed. M. Douglas Meeks (Kingswood Books, 1995), 65–96. For broader reflection on the Wesleys' ministry among the poor, see Richard P. Heitzenrater, ed., *The Poor and the People Called Methodists 1729–1999* (Kingswood Books, 2002). For an overview of the roots of their work among the poor at Oxford, see Richard P. Heitzenrater, *Wesley and the People Called Methodists*, 2nd ed. (Abingdon, 2013), 44–48.

25 John Wesley, "Upon Our Lord's Sermon on the Mount, Discourse 6," in *WJW*, vol. 5, 3rd ed. (Baker Books, 1872), 328.

26 John Wesley, "The Means of Grace," in *WJW*, 5:185–201. In this sermon, Wesley enumerated three practices, yet expanded this list to five in later writings. For analysis, see Tom Schwanda, "Evangelical Spiritual Disciplines," in *Journal of Spiritual Formation and Soul Care* 10, no. 2 (2017): 223 (pp. 220–236). See also the analysis by Fred Sanders, *Wesley on the Christian Life* (Crossway, 2013), 173–189.

27 Wesley, "Means of Grace," in *WJW*, 5:185.

these standard "devotional" acts were to be used alongside works of mercy, as Wesley reckoned both sorts of activities as means of grace that formed believers.[28]

Drawing his text from Matthew 25:36, "I was sick, and ye visited me," Wesley lamented the blindness of many professing Christians to the practical works of care for the poor and imprisoned. Such blindness to the needs of the poor also blinded them to their own spiritual declension, for in neglecting these good works, they were neglecting one of God's ordained means for spiritual strength and health (cf. Eph 2:10).[29] Christians who were scrupulous with regard to devotion but slack in works of mercy might find themselves perplexed during periods of spiritual weakness, for merciful acts were "essentially necessary" to their spiritual health and salvation. Such visits ought to be made personally, by those in all stations of life, with intention to relive the physical and spiritual needs of those visited. Though Wesley proposed limiting his sermon to visiting the "sick," he used "sick" and "poor" as general synonyms throughout the sermon, and such visits clearly presented occasion for the tangible relief of the poor through providing them the "necessaries of life." Christians who made such visits should be prepared to give from their own financial resources, or to appeal to others who could meet these needs.[30]

Acts of mercy such as almsgiving were, in Wesley's economy, more important than acts of piety, and when conflicts between reading or hearing Scripture or prayer and acts of mercy arose, Christians were to prefer mercy over devotion.[31] As Randy Maddox has shown, sermons from Wesley's final decade (1780–1791) contain numerous warnings correlating spiritual decline with growing wealth, rather than distributing charity, among the Methodists.[32]

---

28 John Wesley, "On Visiting the Sick," in *WJW*, vol. 7, 3rd ed. (Grand Rapids: Baker Books, 1872), 117–127.

29 Wesley, "On Visiting the Sick," in *WJW*, 7:117–118.

30 Wesley, "On Visiting the Sick," in *WJW*, 7:121–122.

31 John Wesley, "On Zeal," in *WJW*, 7:57–67 (see esp. pp. 61, 65).

32 See the insightful study of Randy L. Maddox, "'Visit the Poor': John Wesley, the Poor, and the Sanctification of Believers," in *The Poor and the People Called Methodists 1729–1999*, ed. Richard P. Heitzenrater (Kingswood Books, 2002), 62–63 (esp. n. 13).

Mary Lyth

Wesley's emphasis on care for the poor as an act of piety was particularly influential among women who experienced conversion under his ministry. Paul Chilcote summarizes this influence well: "For the women of early Methodism there could be no separation of their personal experience of God and devotion to Christ from their active role as agents of reconciliation and social transformation in the world. Their spirituality was truly incarnational."[33] The work of Mary Lyth of Yorkshire exemplifies this emphasis.

Mary Burdsall Lyth (1782–1860) was a second-generation Methodist. Her mother, also named Mary, was awakened as a teenager through the preaching of her parish priest, began attending secret Methodist meetings, and began witnessing to her family, leading to the conversion of her brothers and household servants. Her father was so troubled by this situation that he threatened to shoot Mary, but decided a better course of action was to fire the servants and banish Mary and her brothers to live at another farm. Quite against her father's wishes, Mary wed Richard Burdsall, a circuit-riding Methodist widower twice her age, and Richard, through persistent ministry, saw his father-in-law converted.[34]

The daughter, Mary, also converted as a teenager, and at the age of fifteen began accompanying other Methodist women to minister among the poor. Reading her private diary entries, published posthumously by her son, one often finds her visiting the poor. Her reflections on this ministry show the impact that this ministry made upon her spiritual life. Caring for the poor helped Mary pursue Christ more deeply:

> I have greater pleasure in visiting the sick and the poor, than in visiting those who, as far as this world is concerned, are better circumstanced; in the former case, my object is simply to do or get good, but in the latter, I find it is in danger of being mixed

---

33 Paul Wesley Chilcote, ed., *Early Methodist Spirituality: Selected Women's Writings* (Kingswood Books, 2007), 31–32.
34 Mary Lyth, *The Blessedness of Religion in Earnest: A Memorial of Mrs. Mary Lyth of York*, ed. John Lyth (Book Society, 1861), 3–11.

with other motives. Christ is the end as well as the source of my happiness. Oh! to be saved in every word and thought, this is what my soul covets. I feel I am getting a firmer hold of Christ.[35]

For Lyth, care for the poor often turned into opportunities for spiritual testimony and evangelism:

> I prayed that the Lord would direct my steps in visiting the poor, and in this He answered me: for quite unexpectedly I was sent for to the bedside of a woman apparently dying, and who, being awakened to her lost condition, lamented the neglect of past opportunities. While a friend was praying, she began to pray for herself, faith instantly sprang up in her heart, and she cried out, "I will believe, Lord help me, I never felt it so with me before."[36]

Mary could include her ministry among the poor alongside other spiritual practices as means of experiencing relational nearness to God: "A day of unusual nearness to God:—in the Lord's house; in visiting the poor; reading the rules of society; and social prayer: although dissatisfied with my performances, I feel I have done what I ought."[37] Her ongoing work among the poor led to Mary's appointment as Treasurer for the Clothing Society, one of many such organizations among the Methodists.[38] She began a York Ladies' Missionary Sewing Meeting to help the cause of global missions, yet it also held devotional importance: "My soul is drawn heavenward. The sewing meeting is much laid upon my mind, that it may improve in spirituality, and that I may fill the post assigned me according to the will of God. I long to spread the savour of Christ among the dear people, and make religion appear more

---

35 Lyth, *Blessedness of Religion*, 67.

36 Lyth, *Blessedness of Religion*, 113.

37 Lyth, *Blessedness of Religion*, 142.

38 Lyth, *Blessedness of Religion*, 191. Apparently Mary Lyth had mixed thoughts about this role, for upon later re-appointment, she described it as a "cross" which she would try to bear (213) and one she ultimately resigned after sixteen years (246).

lovely."[39] For Mary Lyth, a faithful Methodist laywoman in the long eighteenth century, tangible ministry to the poor was spiritually formative.

Jonathan Edwards

One significant reflection on the formative practice of almsgiving comes from the pulpit of Jonathan Edwards.[40] In January 1733, around five years into his Northampton pastorate, Edwards preached four times on Deuteronomy 15:7–11 entitled "The Duty of Charity to the Poor."[41] To put this sermon in context, prior to 1705, Northampton, Massachusetts, then under the pastoral oversight of Edwards's Grandfather Solomon Stoddard, had used public and private funds to care for the poor. The indigent had been housed within the town, and members of the community contributed to meet the financial burdens of the host families. In 1705, the town voted to build a poor house, but it was never constructed.[42]

Edwards declared his doctrine succinctly: "'Tis the most absolute and indispensable duty of a people of God to give bountifully and willingly for the supply of the wants of the needy."[43] Following three relatively brief propositions, Edwards devoted the majority

---

39 Lyth, *Blessedness of Religion*, 187, 234. After nearly two decades of this sewing ministry, Lyth resigned due to ill health, prompting an exchange of letters from the Meeting with Lyth, whose response indicates the strong connection between piety and care for the poor: "I still feel interested in [the Meeting's] prosperity, and if I have one desire above the rest, it is that every one who assists in this good work may not only have her hands employed in it, but her heart enriched by the blessed gospel she wishes to send to heathen lands, and that every effort may have God's approving smile" (247).

40 See the recent treatment of this sermon in Gerald McDermott and Ronald Story, eds., *The Other Jonathan Edwards: Selected Writings on Society, Love, and Justice* (University of Massachusetts Press, 2015).

41 Jonathan Edwards, "The Duty of Charity to the Poor," in *WJE*, vol. 17, *Sermons and Discourses 1730–1733*, ed. Mark Valeri (Yale University Press, 1999), 371–404. The manuscript has four divisions noting where Edwards stopped and started each preaching unit.

42 See McDermott and Story, *Other Jonathan Edwards*, 5.

43 Edwards, "Duty of Charity," in *WJE*, 17:373.

of the sermon to application, raising and identifying eleven objections to providing such care.[44]

Edwards imagined that some hearers would not care for the poor because they recognized themselves as unconverted and thus expected no reward for their actions. Others, he suspected, thought they might slip into a form of works-righteousness by their charity. Still others had become jaded by having cared for the poor previously and not seen the promised blessings of God. Perhaps some chose to withhold charity because the circumstances of their neighbors seemed relatively mild, not desperate or because the poor person had done them wrong in the past. More likely was the thought that some families had little margin to care for their own families, let alone others or that they were not able to discern clearly those who were truly in need. Some were hesitant to give until being asked directly. Others may have reasoned that people were poor because of their own sinful choices and not worthy of care or that other members of the community needed to step up to meet the obligations. Finally, Edwards considered the objection that civic law already made provision for the poor and thus private citizens had no need to help.[45]

For Edwards, almsgiving was an indispensable practice of religion: "'Tis not merely a commendable thing for a man to be kind and bountiful to the poor, but our bounden duty, as much a duty as 'tis to pray or go to meeting, or anything else whatsoever; and the neglect of it brings great guilt upon any person."[46] Later, Edwards reiterated this connection, listing charitable giving alongside Sabbath keeping, prayer, public worship, and Bible reading as duties appointed "to seek God's grace."[47]

Citing Micah 6:8 and James 1:27, Edwards described care for the poor as "one of the greater and more essential duties of religion" and following Christ's own words in Matthew 22:23, as "one

---

44 Application occupies three and a half of the sermon's four preaching units, or around 80 percent of the total sermon. See Mark Valeri's introduction to the sermons in *WJE*, 17:370.

45 Edwards, "Duty of Charity," in *WJE*, 17:390–405.

46 Edwards, "Duty of Charity," in *WJE*, 17:375.

47 Edwards, "Duty of Charity," in *WJE*, 17:390.

of the weightier matters of the law."[48] Furthermore, Edwards acknowledged that such care would be difficult, but answered that "Christ told us the necessity of doing our difficult duties of religion" and that almsgiving was among those difficult duties that marked the "narrow way" of salvation.[49] Appealing to a catena of wisdom and prophetic texts before turning to the New Testament, he asserted that almsgiving "is often mentioned in Scripture as an essential part of the character of a godly man."[50] Almsgiving, for Edwards, was vitally connected to godliness.

Conclusion

While ministry to the poor was spiritually formative for many early evangelicals, for others the connection between almsgiving, or works of mercy, and piety was rarely mentioned. Charles Wesley (1707–1788) gave the topic little attention in his published hymnody.[51] George Whitefield (1714–1770) was heavily involved in works of mercy, notably his Bethesda orphanage in Georgia, and he preached on the topic of benevolence to the poor. However, his writings emphasize the duty of caring for the poor without addressing the inward formation of the believer.[52]

---

48 Edwards, "Duty of Charity," in *WJE*, 17:375.

49 Edwards, "Duty of Charity," in *WJE*, 17:381.

50 Edwards, "Duty of Charity," in *WJE*, 17:381–183. Here Edwards cites Pss 37:21, 26; 112:5, 9; Prov 14:31; 21:26; Isa 57:1; 1 John 3:17–19; 2 Cor 8:8; Matt 25:34–46.

51 Wesley did address care for the poor in two of his Scripture hymns; see Charles Wesley, *Short Hymns on Select Passages of the Holy Scriptures*, vol. 2 (Farley, 1762), 140–141. Hymns 55–57 address Matt 6:1–5. See also Hymn 244, drawn from Matt 26:11. In his hymn "Primitive Christianity," Wesley alluded to the common concern for the poor demonstrated in Acts 2: "Propriety was there unknown/none called what he possess'd his own/where all the common blessing share/no selfish happiness was there." See Charles Wesley, "Primitive Christianity," in *An Earnest Appeal to Men of Reason and Religion*, by John Wesley, 2nd ed. (Farley, 1743), 52.

52 See George Whitefield, *The Great Duty of Charity Recommended, Particularly to all who Profess Christianity* (London, 1740). This sermon is the most extensive in Whitefield's corpus on the topic. Elsewhere, Whitefield described almsgiving as "an excellent curb upon avarice," yet used almsgiving as a foil to warn hearers against false teachers who distorted biblical teachings on such practices.

More research on this topic remains to be done. One avenue of exploration might be early evangelical reception of late Puritan and Pietist authors who joined piety and social action. Charles Hambrick-Stowe does not mention almsgiving as one of the seventeenth century hallmarks of New England Puritan devotion in his incisive study of colonial spirituality, yet it is present among some of the authors he considered.[53] For instance, it might be fruitful to explore any influence that Boston's Cotton Mather had via his *Bonifacius* (1710), or "Essays to do Good," which link days of pastoral prayer and almsgiving, or through his sermons that mention almsgiving among other means of grace.[54] German Pietist August Hermann Francke's sermon "The Duty to the Poor" (1697) uses the biblical example of Cornelius (Acts 10) to encourage rulers to care for the poor and thus to inspire their subjects to imitate their piety.[55] Richard Lovelace has shown how influential Francke was for Mather. How might this emphasis have affected colonial readers, especially in the middle colonies where the presence of German immigrants was more significant than in New England? Though some early evangelicals emphasized the formative nature of almsgiving while others did not, few seem to have ignored the topic of care for the poor altogether. The reason was, and is, that almsgiving is a biblical theme, and a movement that values Scripture cannot easily ignore its importance.

See idem, "The Folly and Danger of Not Being Righteous Enough," in *WGW*, vol. 5 (London, 1772), 150. Whitefield omitted acts of mercy such as almsgiving from his list of the means of grace in his sermon "Walking with God," in *WGW*, 5:21–37.

53 See Charles E. Hambrick-Stowe, *The Practice of Piety: Puritan Devotional Disciplines in Seventeenth-Century New England* (University of North Carolina Press, 1982). Hambrick-Stowe does mention collection for the poor among public ordinances of worship (p. 94).

54 Cotton Mather, *Bonifacius* (Boston, 1701), 101–102, 145; idem, *The Everlasting Gospel* (Boston, 1700), 29. Richard Lovelace, in his study of Mather's spirituality, mentions this sermon in connection with the earlier writings of Thomas Shepherd and the later writings of Jonathan Edwards. See Richard F. Lovelace, "Christian Experience in the Theology of Cotton Mather" (ThD diss., Princeton Theological Seminary, 1968), 190.

55 See August Hermann Francke, "The Duty of Care to the Poor," in *God's Glory, Neighbor's Good: A Brief Introduction to the Writings of August Hermann Francke*, ed. Gary R. Sattler (Covenant, 1982), 155–185.

How an Improper Paradigm for Giving Harms the Poor: Toward a Biblical Understanding of Christian Giving

David A. Croteau

FOR THOSE WHO BELIEVE in the authority of Scripture, the ultimate question regarding Christian giving is what the Scripture says on the topic. However, experiential arguments have been utilized for years to advocate a mandated 10 percent contribution be made to the local church. While these claims will be discussed and answered, examples of how an improper understanding of tithing in the Bible has caused great harm to the poor has been largely ignored in this debate. Proper biblical teaching on Christian giving will alleviate the potentially damaging paradigm of storehouse tithing.[1]

The Definition of Tithing

One of the most important aspects of the debate over the obligation for Christians to tithe is about the exact definition of tithing in the Bible.[2] The word tithe itself means 10 percent. However, an English dictionary does not end the debate on what Scripture says about the practice of tithing. In order to understand how Jews living during Jesus's lifetime would have understood tithing, an understanding of what the Old Testament says is vital.

1 A recent article with a similar conclusion was just published by Craig L. Blomberg: "Ten Percent Won't Work for Everyone," *Christianity Today*, 28 September 2021, https://www.christianitytoday.com/pastors/2021/fall/ten-percent-wont-work-everyone-tithe-blomberg.html

2 For more detailed analysis on tithing and Christians, see David A. Croteau, *You Mean I Don't Have to Tithe? A Deconstruction of Tithing and a Reconstruction of Post-Tithe Giving* (Pickwick, 2010); idem, ed., *Perspectives on Tithing: 4 Views* (Broadman & Holman, 2011); idem, *Tithing after the Cross* (Energion, 2013).

Tithing in Mosaic law was defined as giving 10 percent of one's increase from crops grown in the Land of Israel or cattle that feed off the land of Israel. The tithe was connected to the land of Israel, and it never referred to an increase in capital that occurred apart from the land. Israelites gave a tithe multiple times during a year and the total amount tithed was probably at least 20 percent.

Numbers 18:21 commands that Israelites give 10 percent of the increase of their crops from the land to the Levites. According to Leviticus 27:30–32, three items were liable to tithing: seed of the land, fruit of the tree, and animals from the herd or flock. Scholars refer to this as the Levitical tithe.

Deuteronomy 14:22–27 describes a second tithe, the festival tithe. The purpose of this tithe was to provide a financial base for celebrating three festivals: Passover, Tabernacles, and Pentecost (or, the Festival of Weeks). Crops and cattle are both liable to the festival tithe.

Deuteronomy 14:28–29 describes the charity tithe. This tithe is given every three years. The following chart illustrates the pattern of tithing described in the Mosaic law:

Year 1	Levitical tithe and festival tithe
Year 2	Levitical tithe and festival tithe
Year 3	Levitical tithe, festival tithe, and charity tithe
Year 4	Levitical tithe and festival tithe
Year 5	Levitical tithe and festival tithe
Year 6	Levitical tithe, festival tithe, and charity tithe

Since every seventh year was supposed to be a Sabbatical Year, nothing was required to be given. From this, it appears that the giving percentage by year was as follows:

Year 1	20 percent
Year 2	20 percent
Year 3	30 percent
Year 4	20 percent
Year 5	20 percent
Year 6	30 percent
Year 7	0 percent

If this is accurate, then the average percentage given from crops and cattle in a seven-year cycle is 20 percent (23.33 percent if only including years 1 through 6). While other required offerings are commanded in the Mosaic law, calculating how those would fit into a percentage of giving of one's increase is not realistic and is not included.

Furthermore, calculating the exact percentage to be given yearly is more complicated than the chart above. Some scholars believe that the charity tithe would replace the festival tithe (or maybe the Levitical tithe) in years 3 and 6 of the seven-year cycle. However, there are two main problems with that view. First, if the charity tithe replaced the festival tithe, then there would be no way to celebrate the festivals during those years. Second, if the charity tithe replaced the Levitical tithe, then the Levites would not be adequately supported during those years. The exact percentage given is still a more complicated issue.

Contrary to popular belief, the Israelites were only commanded to give about 20 percent of the produce of *crops and cattle*, but they were never required to give from income apart from that. Some interpreters have countered that Israel was an agricultural society. While that is true, many Israelites had professions that were not primarily agricultural. Tubal-Cain, for example, was a blacksmith (see Gen 4:22). Some Israelites were carpenters or fishermen, and their primary income was not connected to agriculture. According to the Mosaic law, income earned from a profession not connected to cattle or crops was not liable to the laws of tithing.

One final complicating factor should be mentioned. When the Levitical tithe requires 10 percent of cattle to be tithed, the specific description of how this was accomplished actually results in 10 percent rarely being given. Leviticus 27:32 says, "Every tenth animal from the herd or flock, which passes under the shepherd's rod, will be holy to the LORD" (CSB). Therefore, if an Israelite had ten sheep, the tenth sheep that passed under the rod would be liable to tithing: 10 percent. But, if an Israelite had nine sheep, zero would be given. If they had nineteen sheep, only one would be given: about 5.3 percent. It is actually impossible to calculate what percentage of income an Israelite was required to give in order to obey the Mosaic law because the percentage would be different for everyone and every year.[3]

Pro-Tithing Experiential Arguments

There are many ways that scholars and pastors have argued that Christians are mandated to give 10 percent of their income to the local church (or, storehouse tithing). Most of the arguments are either biblical, theological, or historical. Experiential or pragmatic arguments have also proved to be powerful arguments. Three significant experiential arguments will be defined and a response will be provided.

The Anecdotal Argument

Moody Press published a book in 1960 that contained letters of people who were blessed by God after they started tithing.[4] The purpose for the book was to demonstrate that God would always provide for those who doubted their financial ability to tithe and/ or whether it was a biblical requirement. The anecdotal argument: God proves that tithing is the current requirement for Christians by significantly blessing those who are faithful in tithing.[5] In fact, some ministries have offered to give "refunds" to church members who try tithing if they are not better off financially after a certain time period. In fact, one preacher proclaimed that no one has ever gone bankrupt while tithing!

In reality, many people have gone bankrupt while tithing. President Bill Clinton signed a law in 1998 to protect tithing under the federal bankruptcy code.[6] This was a response to several lawsuits

---

3 More could be said about different tithes in the Mosaic law, like the priestly tithe, but they are not overly important for this discussion.

4 Anonymous, *I Tithe Joyfully! A Book of Letters from Those Who Do* (Moody, 1960).

5 Ralph S. Cushman and Martha F. Bellinger, *Adventures in Stewardship* (Abingdon, 1919), 11.

6 Chuck Grassley, "Religious Liberty and Charitable Donation Project Act of 1998," 20 June 1998, https://www.grassley.senate.gov/news/news-releases/religious-liberty-and-charitable-donation-protect-act-1998.

filed by creditors trying to recapture money given to churches while people were tithing when going bankrupt.[7] The reason the federal government has been involved in this issue is evidence that the problem with tithers going bankrupt was not uncommon.

It is true that many people's financial situation does appear to improve when they start tithing. One reason for this could be that when someone is trying to learn how to live off of 10 percent less of their income, they become more meticulous and aware of how they are spending their money. This will naturally make them better stewards of their resources. In the end, they are "blessed" because they are obeying biblical principles of stewardship, not because they are obeying a biblical mandate.

This argument has proved to be very powerful on the poor around the world. Many impoverished people have been told that if they start to tithe, God promises to bless them (cf. Mal 3:8–10). On a trip to India several years ago, I was told about a prominent preacher who visited the country and used this argument to convince impoverished Christians to give to his ministry. He was so compelling, that they stopped giving to their church and started giving to his ministry. These Christians were never financially blessed, and hundreds upon hundreds of churches shut down as a result. The poor became poorer, and the church in India was weakened.

The Concession Argument

At least three prominent Christian leaders in church history have utilized the concession argument: John Chrysostom, Jerome, and Augustine. The concession argument: the biblical mandate is to sell all your possessions and give the proceeds to the poor (cf. Matt 19:21; Mark 10:22; Luke 18:22); since most Christians will not be

---

7 See, e.g., Religious News Service, "U.S. Goes after Bankrupt Couple's Church Donations," *Chicago Tribune*, 20 May 1994, https://www.chicagotribune.com/news/ct-xpm-1994-05-20-9405200024-story.html. For more information on this issue, including a temporary overruling of this based upon the Bankruptcy Abuse Prevention and Consumer Protection Act of 2005, see anonymous, "House Passes Law to Protect Tithing in Bankruptcy," *InsideArm*, 8 December 2006, http://www.insidearm.com/news/00007829-house-passes-law-to-protect-tithing-in-ba.

willing to live up to the biblical standard, they should at least give as Jews gave under the Mosaic law, that is, 10 percent.

Jerome concluded that Jesus's statement in Luke 18:22 was for every Christian, but since Christians are unwilling to obey this command, they should "imitate the rudimentary teaching of the Jews" and give 10 percent of their income to support the clergy and the poor.[8] Augustine's and Chrysostom's arguments were similar.[9]

There are two primary responses to this argument. First, if the command in Luke 18:22 is an actual mandate for every Christian today, then no one has the authority to lower the standard of the command. If Luke 18:22 was intended to be a command for every Christian and Scripture is truly the authority for faith and practice, then on what basis could anyone justify lowering that standard? The command to sell everything and give the proceeds to the poor is not a universal command for Christians today. Jesus was speaking to a particular man in a particular situation. Paying careful attention to the context of Luke 18:22, Blomberg says, "In Luke two stories follow closely on the heels of this episode (Luke 18:18–30) that prove Jesus makes different demands of different individuals."[10] Blomberg then refers to the story of Zaccheus (Luke 19:1–10) who gives away half his income, not all of it. Then he mentions the parable of the talents (Luke 19:11–27) where Jesus exhorts his disciples to invest their money wisely. Blomberg concludes, "But in each of these passages, Jesus commands Christians to use all their possessions, not just some fixed percentage of them, for kingdom priorities."[11]

Second, the argument by concession assumes that tithing in the

---

8 John Sharp, "Tithes," in *Dictionary of Christian Antiquities*, ed. William Smith and Samuel Cheetham (John Murray, 1893), 2:1664. Jerome also commends Christians to tithe in his *Commentary on Matthew* 2.22 (cited by Stuart Murray, *Beyond Tithing* [Paternoster, 2000], 117).

9 Augustine, *On the Psalms: Psalm 147*, 13 (NPNF1 8:668). In Augustine's writings, he discussed the scribes and Pharisees, for the most part, as if they gave only 10 percent. See comments in Augustine, *Sermon 35* (NPNF1 6:367–368); *Sermon 56* (NPNF1 6:435–436). See also comments in Justo González, *Faith and Wealth* (Harper, 1990), 219. John Chrysostom, *Homily IV: Homilies on Ephesians* (NPNF1 13:69); *Gospel of Mathew* 64.4 (NPNF1 10:395–396).

10 Craig Blomberg, *Matthew*, NAC 22 (Broadman & Holman, 1992), 298.

11 Blomberg, *Matthew*, 299.

Old Testament was defined as giving 10 percent of one's income. As discussed above, this simply is not true.

The Pragmatic Argument

Many pastors have noted that apart from saying to a member of their church to give 10 percent of their income, they would have nothing specific and helpful to say in guiding them on how to give. The pragmatic argument: the method of tithing is very easy to understand.[12] The calculation is simple, just take your paycheck and multiply it by 0.1. Not only is it easy to understand, it can be done very systematically: every time you have an increase (like receiving a paycheck), you give to the church.

This argument implies that tithing must be taught to church members because there is no other paradigm to replace it. While some books have been written to tear down the mandated tithing paradigm without an attempt to replace it with another model, there are many principles in Scripture to guide Christian giving that have no connection to tithing.

While it is true that the paradigm for giving that will be mentioned later is more complicated than giving 10 percent of income, it will, at the same time, demonstrate that there are many principles given in Scripture to guide giving. These principles, when properly applied, will draw people into a closer relationship with their God. Easy is not always better, and easy is not always biblical. And these principles will protect the poor from placing a burden of giving upon them that God never intended.

How Improper Paradigms Have Been Injurious to the Poor

The following stories are a few specific examples of how requiring the poor to tithe is harmful. While experiential arguments should never rule the day, they are instructive on how some Christian

---

12 See the following interpreters for this argument: Leewin B. Williams, *Financing the Kingdom* (Eerdmans, 1945), 42; J. E. Dillard, *Good Stewards* (Broadman, 1953), 90–91; Luther P. Powell, *Money and the Church* (Association Press, 1962), 224–225.

leaders are using this improper paradigm for giving in a way that is very destructive to poor Christians.

In 2005, Loretta Davis was a 65-year-old wheelchair-bound woman and a member of The Living Word Tabernacle in Waverly, Ohio. Her income was $592 per month from Social Security. She contributed $60 every month to the church, her tithe plus a small offering. But in January of 2005 after having open heart surgery, she started suffering from cellulitis, a bacterial skin infection that can cause serious health problems. She was in and out of the hospital fifteen times during the first six or seven months of the year. The church revoked her membership because she stopped tithing during these months. In reaction to this, her 83-year-old mother left the church.[13] The approach to giving taken by the leadership of that church was harmful to Loretta Davis and her mother. In fact, 1 Timothy 5:1–16 explains that in some circumstances, the church should be taking care of widows, making sure their needs are met. Instead of taking care of Loretta Davis, the church revoked her membership.

In a 2009 news article, the reporter described a very disturbing situation occurring in Nigeria. He explained that churches were started as a means of financial gain for pastors, like an investment. They were designed as "a means of looting the poor" and that the poor were unable to differentiate fake and legitimate commands of the Bible.[14] This is the shocking part: "No wonder ladies are going into fornication and/or prostitution in order to pay their tithes and offerings."[15] Admittedly, this sounds sensationalistic, but yet this was the report. This is an astounding example of how an improper paradigm for giving can harm the poor, particularly when it is matched with manipulative teaching.

There are several stories of people who have been fired because

---

13 Anonymous, "Wheelchair-Bound Woman Kicked Out of Church: Dismissal Turns into Talk of Ohio Town," *NBC4i*, 15 July 2005, https://web.archive.org/web/20060303050644/https://www.nbc4i.com/news/4727464/detail.html.

14 Anonymous, "African Women Prostitute Themselves to Afford 'Tithes,'" *AllAfrica.com*, May 5, 2009, https://web.archive.org/web/20090603082428/http://groupsects.wordpress.com/2009/05/05/african-women-prostitute-themselves-to-afford-tithes.

15 Anonymous, "African Women Prostitute Themselves to Afford 'Tithes.'"

they failed to tithe. Sometimes the reason for not tithing is theological, but sometimes it is because the person simply could not afford to give 10 percent of their income.[16]

The Most Significantly Abused Passage: Malachi 3:8–10

Malachi 3:8–10 is probably the most well-known passage on tithing, and it is used, by some, in a very manipulative manner. Robert Morris, pastor of Gateway Church in Southlake, Texas, is one of the most popular pro-tithing preachers of the last decade. In discussing Malachi 3, Morris says that Christians who do not tithe are under a curse: "God says, 'You've stolen from me. You've robbed me and because of that, you're under a curse and I don't want you under a curse. I don't want you living under a curse, but you're voluntarily placing yourself under a curse because you're going away from my ordinary principles of behavior." In a separate message, he clarifies, at least in part, what being under that curse includes when he declares that non-tithers are opening the door to demons.[17] Can this understanding of Malachi 3 be justified?[18]

---

16 For example, Carolyn Jackson was fired for failure to tithe. See Baird Helgeson, "Church Employee Says She Lost Job Once Tithing Dipped," *Tampa Tribune*, 23 September 2009, https://web.archive.org/web/20090926143835/http://www2.tbo.com/content/2009/sep/23/church-employee-says-she-lost-job-once-tithing-dip/news-breaking. Kevin Rohr was apparently fired for not tithing. See Suzanne Sataline, "The Backlash against Tithing," *Wall Street Journal*, 23 November 2007, https://www.wsj.com/articles/SB119576921737201375. Another story that caused a lawsuit is no longer available on the internet: Jeffrey Simpson, "Salvation Army's 11th-hour Settlement: Man Who Claims He Was Fired for Not Tithing Granted Year's Salary," *Chronicle Herald*, 8 April 2006, http://thechronicleherald.ca/Front/495572.html (the page that has been taken down).

17 Exit Churchianity, "'Non-tithers OPEN THE DOOR TO DEMONS!!' Says False Teacher Robert Morris," 8 October 2013, YouTube video, 1:11, https://www.youtube.com/watch?v=Hu_Zl6c0nF4.

18 For others who have used Malachi 3 to advocate for the requirement of Christians to tithe, see Jerome (cited by Sharp, "Tithes," 2:1664); George D. Watson, *Soul Food: Being Chapters on the Interior Life with Passages of Personal Experience* (Knapp, 1896), 98; Frank H. Leavell, *Training in Stewardship* (Sunday School Board Southern Baptist Convention, 1920), 64; Stephen Olford, *The Grace of Giving: Thoughts on Financial Stewardship* (Zondervan, 1972), 28–29; Larry Burkett, *Giving and Tithing* (Moody, 1991), 36; William D. Watley, *Bring*

Malachi 3 appears to be discussing the Levitical tithe of Numbers 18:21.[19] Israel is told that they are robbing God of "tithes and offerings." The tithe intended to support the Levites and priests was not being given as commanded in the Mosaic law. In contemporary usage, many Christians use "offerings" as if they were non-obligatory contributions. But Malachi 3 referred to required contributions as prescribed in the Mosaic law. Verhoef comments that the offering "was not taken from the cereal offering, or from the sin offerings, these being most sacred, but from the peace offerings and other sacred gifts, in the form of the breast of the wave offering, the thigh of the ram of ordination (Exod 29:27, 28; etc.), cakes of leavened bread, etc. (Lev 7:14). It was one of the chief sources of the priests' livelihood."[20] They were used to support the temple staff. These "tithes and offerings" were supposed to be brought to the "storehouse."

The reference to the "storehouse" is usually interpreted today as a reference to the local church. But Malachi was referring to an actual building used by the Levites to store the tithes and offerings they received. The storehouse does not find its design in the Mosaic law, but was built for pragmatic reasons as discussed in 2 Chronicles 31:10–12. This makes the connection between the "storehouse" and the "local church" unlikely.

Malachi 3:10 contains a reference to "test" God. Many contemporary preachers will tell their congregations that this offer to test God is still valid, and they use this to challenge Christians to try tithing to see if God is still faithful. But the offer to test God occurs in the context of the Mosaic covenant. The blessings and curses of Deuteronomy 28 are still in full effect when Malachi wrote these words. The offer to test God is modified by the phrase "in this" (NASB). So Malachi does not state this testing in universal terms, but he limits the test to the current situation.[21]

---

the Full Tithe: Sermons on the Grace of Giving (Judson, 1995), 7.

19 Some interpreters might think that Malachi is still addressing the priests, but it appears that he has shifted and is now addressing all of Israel. If he was still addressing the priests, then the tithe under discussion would be the festival tithe.

20 Pieter Verhoef, The Books of Haggai and Malachi, NICOT (Eerdmans, 1987), 305.

21 Daniel I. Block says that "in this" may refer to "in this context" or "at

Three blessings are promised to those who tithed: the first promise is of rain, the second promise is to prevent locusts from destroying crops, and the third promise is for abundant crops. Rather than allegorizing these promises for today, Smith's wise conclusion should be considered: "It may be that this passage in Malachi should be understood as a one-time, special act on God's part to renew the fires of faith in an age of skepticism and indifference. If so, then this is not an open-ended promise to bless in a material way anyone and everyone who tithes his possessions."[22]

If this passage is consistently applied to the church today, then offerings[23] are not freewill and voluntary, but required just like tithes. Therefore, if a Christian today were to give only 10 percent of their income to the local church (not that the Jews only gave 10 percent), then they would still be in sin for robbing God of His offerings. However, how much would an offering be today in monetary terms? This question is virtually impossible to answer. The nature of an offering means it is nearly impossible to calculate a dollar amount or percentage amount for today. Therefore, Malachi 3, monetarily, is not transferrable into the new covenant.[24]

Gospel-Driven Giving

In *Tithing after the Cross*, I described eighteen principles that should guide Christian giving.[25] Here I will discuss two categories of giving: the driving force of giving and the amount of giving. Many Christians desire to get right to the question of "how much should I give" or "what percentage should I give?"[26] However, several principles should be understood before the question of

---

this moment." Daniel I. Block, "Tithe, Tenth" (course notes, Southeastern Baptist Theological Seminary, 2003).

22 Ralph L. Smith, *Micah–Malachi*, WBC 32 (Word, 1984), 334.

23 Many tithing advocates refer to offerings as the freewill or voluntary portion of giving that occurs after someone has tithed.

24 For a discussion on how Malachi 3 does apply to Christians, see Croteau, *You Mean I Don't Have to Tithe?*, 126.

25 Croteau, *Tithing after the Cross*, chap. 7 ("Giving after the Cross").

26 For an interesting discussion, see D. A. Carson, "Are Christians Required to Tithe?," *Christianity Today* 43, no. 13 (November 1999): 94.

amount is answered. Christian giving is an act of worship. Worshipping God and bringing glory to Him in all that we do should penetrate every area of our lives.

The Driving Force of Giving

Many years ago I attended a church that sent out an email in late December to remind the members that they needed to drop off at the church office any last-minute contributions if they wanted it to count on their taxes for that year. Church was cancelled the last Sunday of the year because of an ice storm. Regardless, the contributions received that week were more than any other Sunday the entire year. The motivation for giving that week appeared to be receiving a tax break. While there is nothing wrong with getting a tax break, Scripture provides other driving forces for Christian giving.

The three driving forces for giving can all be found in 2 Corinthians 8–9. First, Christian giving should be grace-driven. Giving is a response to the grace of God shown to believers. The concepts of giving and grace are the overarching themes tying together 2 Corinthians 8–9. In fact, the Greek word for grace (*charis*) is used eighteen times in 2 Corinthians, and ten of those eighteen uses are in these two chapters. Paul begins this section in 8:1 by framing the discussion about the sacrificial and generous giving by the Macedonians by referring to their giving as "the grace of God." Their contributions to help the poor saints in Jerusalem are described as an "act of grace" three times (2 Cor 8:6, 7, 19). How can God's grace become a driving force in Christian giving?

Christians need to take time frequently to meditate on God's grace. The more a Christian dwells on the gospel and recognizes that they have done nothing to earn salvation, nothing whatsoever to work their way into a right relationship with God, that they were utterly dead in their trespasses and sins before God initiated a relationship with them, then the more thankful and grateful they will become. God did not merely sprinkle His grace upon the Christian, for 2 Corinthians 9:14 refers to the "surpassing grace of God." BDAG declares that the Greek word for surpassing refers to "a degree that extraordinarily exceeds a point on a scale of extent."[27] When a Christian begins to truly grasp the extent of God's grace poured out upon them, it will create a well of thankfulness and drive the Christian to worship God in their giving. Therefore, God's grace should be a primary driving force in giving.

Second, Christian giving should be relationship-driven: giving is based upon one's relationship with the Lord. Paul says that the Macedonians gave themselves first "to the Lord" (2 Cor 8:5). This is not a reference to temporal sequence, but mainly to priority or prominence. A Christian's relationship with Christ should be placed above every aspect of their lives. Spending time with the Lord, seeking wisdom from the Lord, praising the Lord for all the blessings He has poured out upon them, and adoring Him for who He is, this will cause change. This is why Paul can declare in 2 Cor 8:8 that generous giving is a demonstration of the genuineness of a Christians love for God. An intimate relationship with Christ will drive generous Christian giving.

Third, Christian giving should be love-driven. Giving is a demonstration of a Christian's love. The concept of love in 2 Cor 8:8–9 provides an example of giving that is driven by love. Jesus gave of Himself. Without love, giving everything one has results in nothing (cf. 1 Cor 13:3). When Jesus died on the cross, He provided the ultimate demonstration of love (cf. 1 John 4:9–10). When a Christian meditates on the grace of God, as a Christian pursues God with all their heart, soul, mind, and strength, God will fill them with love so that they can pour this love out on those around them. Generous giving is a manifestation of Christian love. John Mueller concludes: "It is only at the foot of the blood-stained cross of Calvary that the believer learns the art of Christian giving."[28] Love for Christ will drive Christian giving.

The Amount of Giving

When teaching through the eighteen principles of Christian

---

27 BDAG, 1032.
28 John Theodore Mueller, *Christian Dogmatics: A Handbook of Doctrinal Theology for Pastors, Teachers, and Laymen* (Concordia, 1934), 415.

giving, the last category discussed is the amount of giving. This, at times, frustrates Christians. This is the moment of truth where all the previous principles on giving are applied to the Christian life or are ignored. Sometimes, the question asked seems to imply: "How little can I give and not be sinning?" When the question implies that, it reveals a heart-disposition of someone who has not truly imbibed the previous fourteen principles.

Christianity is not very formulaic; it is more relational. A person does not get saved by repeating a magical formula. Similarly, the amount a particular Christian should give cannot be dictated by the use of a calculator alone. Four final principles need to be considered regarding the amount of giving.

First, the amount given should be based upon income. Proportionate giving means that the value of the contribution is expected to be related to the income of the giver. This principle can be found in Deut 16:17 where Moses said that the gift should be "according to the blessing the LORD your God has given you" (CSB). Paul expresses the same concept in 1 Cor 16:2 when he says that the amount of the gift should be based on "the extent that God has blessed you" (NET; see also 2 Cor 8:12).

The more one has been blessed, the greater proportion the gift should be. The percentage of income given by someone making $20,000 per year should be lower than someone making $60,000 per year.[29] However, Empty Tomb research has demonstrated that those making $5,000–$39,000 per year give more proportionately than those making $40,000–$150,000+.[30] More recently, while giving in 1968 among church members averaged 3.02 percent, by 2018 it had declined to 2.05 percent.[31]

Second, a Christian should consider the needs of those ministering to them and the needs of fellow saints. Paul explains that preachers of the gospel have the right to be supported (1 Cor

---

29 Obviously, exceptional circumstances occur. But this is a general principle.

30 See Empty Tomb, Inc., "Income Bracket Highlights," 2007, https://web.archive.org/web/20090611134634/http://www.emptytomb.org/05cesincome.html.

31 RNS Press Release Distribution Service, "Long-Term Declines in Church Giving and Membership Can Be Addressed," *Religious News Service*, 13 April 2021, https://religionnews.com/2021/04/13/long-term-declines-in-church-giving-and-membership-can-be-addressed.

9:1–14; cf. Gal 6:6). This means that the needs of the pastoral staff at the local church should be considered when giving. This principle does not justify a minister making an exorbitant amout of money. One of the qualifications of an elder is that they are not a lover of money (1 Tim 3:3) or not greedy for gain (Titus 1:7).

The needs of other saints should be considered as well. Paul refers to this twice in 2 Corinthians. He says in 8:13–14 that God supplied an abundance of resources to the Corinthians in order for them to meet the needs of the saints in Jerusalem. Then he adds in 9:12 that the collection will be used for "supplying the needs of the saints" (CSB). A Christian should consider the needs of those ministering to them and the needs of fellow Christians when deciding on an amount to give.

Third, Christian giving should be generous, but not to the point of personal affliction. The word typically translated "generosity" in 2 Corinthians 8:2 is usually translated "sincerity" or "simplicity." The meaning in this context is helpfully explained by David Garland: "It comes to mean generosity as those with a singleness of concern for another's need stand ready to help."[32] The Macedonians surely gave generously, as should Christians today. However, the concept of generous should be tempered with wisdom. Paul affirms in 2 Corinthians 8:3 that the Macedonians gave "beyond their ability" (CSB), but he also says that he does not want "relief for others and hardship for" the Corinthians (2 Cor 8:13 [CSB]).[33]

Fourth, the amount given is to be heart-based. God tells Moses in Exodus 25 that he needs to raise a contribution from the Israelites to construct a tabernacle. Moses speaks to Israel and asks for those whose hearts are willing (cf. Exod 35:5) to participate in the contribution. The Israelite giving was overwhelming: "everyone whose heart was moved … all who had willing hearts" (Exod 35:21–22 CSB). The contribution from the Israelites was so overwhelmingly generous that Moses needed to command all contributions cease in Exodus 36:6. Paul says in 2 Corinthians 9:7 that

---

32 David E. Garland, *2 Corinthians*, NAC 29 (Broadman, 1999), 367.

33 I have personally witnessed friends give so much to those in need that they had to turn to their church for financial help. Paul is warning against this form of unwise giving.

a Christian should give "as he has decided in his heart" (CSB). BDAG explains that this phrase means "as he has made up in his mind."[34] Barnett concluded "careful prior deliberation by the giver is implied by these instructions."[35] God wants the Christian to dedicate themselves to Him first, and then He will move their hearts and lead them in generous, sacrificial giving. The gospel should be the driving force for Christian giving, not a calculator.

Giving and the Poor

Those who desire to remain with the mandated storehouse tithing paradigm should reflect upon Proverbs 22:16: "Oppressing the poor to enrich oneself, and giving to the rich—both lead only to poverty" (CSB). The laws on tithing in the Old Testament are not irrelevant to concepts for Christian giving. Not every Israelite was required to tithe. If you did not own land, you had no increase in cattle that fed from the Land nor crops that grew from the Land. Only landowners were required to tithe. So the poorest of the Israelites would not be involved in giving in the tithing system. Instead, the poor actually received tithe money in the Old Testament. The Charity Tithe was intended for the Levite, the resident alien, the fatherless, and the widow (Deut 14:29).

The offerings discussed in Leviticus 1 are instructive as well. Roy Gane notes that the "sacrificial victims [in Leviticus 1] are logically presented in descending order of size and value."[36] Animals from the herd were most valuable (Lev 1:2–9), animals from the flock were next in value (Lev 1:10–13), and birds were the least valuable (Lev 1:14–17). Mark Rooker concludes that "the type of sacrifice presented would correspond to the donor's ability and resources," those who had some means would present a bull for an offering, average Israelites would offer a sheep, and the poor would offer a bird. God recognizes that the poor will desire to honor Him,

---

34 BDAG, 865.

35 Paul Barnett, *The Second Epistle to the Corinthians*, NICNT (Eerdmans, 1997), 437.

36 Roy E. Gane, "Leviticus," in *Zondervan Illustrated Bible Backgrounds Commentary (Old Testament)*, vol. 1, *Genesis, Exodus, Leviticus, Numbers, Deuteronomy*, ed. John H. Walton (Zondervan, 2009), 289.

but he makes accommodations for their contributions. The mandated storehouse tithing model does not account for these concepts very well.

Any model for Christian giving must primarily be based upon Scripture. The mandated storehouse tithing paradigm has created an unfair burden upon the poor. Certain manifestations of this model have been extremely harmful for the poor, but even the best manifestation of this model is still imbalanced.

Carl F. H. Henry, American Capitalism, and Evangelical Engagement

Matthew J. Hall

THROUGHOUT HIS LIFETIME, Carl Henry exhibited a consistent rejection of socialist, communist, or Marxian economic theories and political proposals. Instead, he contended that free enterprise and capitalism were systems worthy of defense and strengthening. And yet, Henry also was quite willing to concede that capitalism was vulnerable to the corruptions of modern secularism in such a way that it could do real harm to human flourishing and the principles of justice found in biblical revelation.

This essay rehearses some of Henry's own wrestling with the social and cultural debates surrounding capitalism in post-war America, as well as the intramural debates within American evangelicalism. In the immediate aftermath of World War II, Henry's vision for an evangelical identity renewed by Christian social action earned scorn from more conservative or fundamentalist critics. In turn, Henry inspired a generation of reformist evangelicals who took his exhortation to heart. However, by the 1970s many of that generation increasingly became critical of Henry for his refusal to concede to the demands of the New Left and demands for more revolutionary fundamental transformations of American economic structures.

In the past decade, historians have retrieved the stories of the shaping influences of prominent industrialists upon the formation of post-war evangelicalism. Their work has helpfully highlighted the ways wealthy laymen leveraged their influence to direct the course of various sectors of the evangelical movement. And yet, sometimes these more recent interpretations have taken too simple a portrait, as if to suggest that evangelical theologians and institutions were largely doing the bidding of a dominant capital class. Because of this overemphasis, at times, their interpretations have flattened evangelicals resulting in a rather monochromatic picture.[1]

While others may have been reflexive apologists for all things big business or capitalist, that was not Carl Henry. In fact, he retained a consistent voice throughout his work—albeit one that modulated somewhat in ways reflective of context—that called for a redemptive center to Christian economics and to capitalism in particular. While he argued strenuously that Marxism was indeed incompatible with Christianity, he conceded that this was not the case with capitalism. Instead, he concluded the two could be reconciled. And yet this was a noticeably different tack than that of evangelical capitalists who were eager to impose the economic system upon any biblical passage available.

Neo-Evangelicalism Ascendant and Henry

From the earliest years of Carl Henry's writing, he exhibited the themes that would dominate his analysis of capitalism and alternative models for decades to come. For example, in his seminal *The Uneasy Conscience of Modern Fundamentalism* (1947), Henry warned of the dangers of communism. As the West emerged from World War II, he wrote,

> Evangelicalism must not make the mistake, so common in our day, of regarding Communism or state Socialism as the adequate rectification of the errors of totalitarianism or the inadequacies of democracism. No political or economic system has utopian promise if the essential redemptive ingredient is missing from it. A redemptive totalitarianism is far preferable

---

1 For example, see Timothy E. W. Gloege, *Guaranteed Pure: The Moody Bible Institute, Business, and the Making of Modern Evangelicalism* (University of North Carolina Press, 2015); Kevin M. Kruse, *One Nation under God: How Corporate America Invented Christian America* (Basic, 2015); Darren E. Grem, *The Blessings of Business: How Corporations Shaped Conservative Christianity* (Oxford University Press, 2016); Darren Dochuk, *Anointed with Oil: How Christianity and Crude Made Modern America* (Basic, 2019).

to an unredemptive democracy; a redemptive Communism far more advantageous than an unredemptive Capitalism, and vice versa.[2]

This encapsulates much of the core of Henry's thinking on the subject over the next half century. At the core of his analysis was a concern for the prioritization of the redemptive essence of the gospel and the realities of the kingdom of Christ. If that redemptive essence were hollowed out from any social, political, or economic system, it would inevitably lead to civilizational decay and eventual ruin. This emphasis placed Henry on sometimes difficult to situate ground. He would never give quarter to those who would seek to undermine free enterprise or propose Marxist alternatives. And yet, he refused to play by the rules of some of capitalism's most ardent boosters within American evangelicalism.

While some have thus argued that Henry charted a centrist course, moderating between Marxian evangelical liberals on one extreme and more fundamentalist reflexive capitalists on the other, that kind of spectrum seems to oversimplify things.[3] Henry found himself critiquing almost everyone, including theonomist reconstructionists and dominionists, Marxian New Left evangelicals calling for revolution, and those on the far right who seemed to traffic in an unquestioned conflation of biblical revelation with modern capitalism. Throughout his life and work, those tension points became apparent in different ways as the social and cultural challenges within evangelicalism evolved.

Evangelicals and Capitalism after World War II

As the evangelical movement boomed in the postwar years, it did so in the context of Eisenhower Republicanism and a soaring GDP. While evangelical leaders were largely of a shared mind in

---

2 Carl F. H. Henry, *The Uneasy Conscience of Modern Fundamentalism* (Eerdmans, 1947), 72.

3 Robert Booth Fowler, *Evangelical Political Thought, 1966–1976* (Eerdmans, 1982), 77–93; Craig Matthew Gay, "Recent Evangelical Appraisals of Capitalism and American Class Culture" (PhD diss., Boston University, 1989), 243–248.

their affirmation of free-market capitalism, there were internal divisions that underscored some of their divergent emphases. Some
of these hit close to home for Carl Henry. For his part, Henry had
steered *Christianity Today* (*CT*) in a particular direction as the
magazine's founding editor in 1956. While not the enterprise's sole
benefactor, one of the magazine's major financial backers was oil
magnate J. Howard Pew. Others have noted the tension that existed
at times between Pew's ambitions for the magazine and Henry's
more measured direction.[4] It says something that Pew was also a
major funder—through his Glen Meade Trust—of *Christian Economics*, a publication of the Christian Freedom Foundation. The
Foundation had been established by Howard Kershner and Nor-
man Vincent Peale. While the latter is likely still familiar to many,
Kershner may be less so. The magazine had been founded in 1950
and took a much more overtly pro-capitalist tone, issuing apologetics for modern capitalism in each fortnightly release.[5]

Kershner was no hack. He'd done quite well for himself after studying economics at Harvard and had been an early critic
of FDR's New Deal policies. One can get a good sampling of his
thought by reading an address he delivered at Pepperdine University in 1958. After mounting a defense of the economic policies
of the Hoover administration, Kershner gave an impassioned defense of the rightful place and virtue of profit in a free society. In
return, he distilled socialism down to theft, thus rendering it to
be an inherently evil economic system and one fundamentally at
odds with biblical truth:

> This is the mainspring of socialism. To have more than one
> himself creates; to get something from what other people do;
> to take something away from them and appropriate it for our-
> selves. Nobody would be a socialist if he didn't think he was
> going to get more out of it than he's getting. If he gets more,
> where does the more come from? From somebody else. It's
> based on covetousness. And the Good Book says to us, "Thou
> shalt not covet." We're rewriting that Commandment today to

---

4 Grem, *The Blessings of Business*, 80.
5 Gay, "Recent Evangelical Appraisals," 52.

read, "Thou shalt not covet except that portion of thy neighbor's wealth which exceeds thine own."[6]

But perhaps no one was more zealous in his pressure than J. Howard Pew. In the years before Pew's death in 1971, it seems clear that internal tensions between the *CT* board—including Pew—and Henry as editor mounted, particularly over the legitimacy of biblical criticism of expressions of capitalism (although there was broader divergence over a range of issues related to social action). Henry's departure from *CT* in 1968 was certainly not an entirely happy one. And Henry's own dissatisfaction with the editorial direction taken by his successor, Harold Lindsell, became quite apparent in the years to follow.

Some of Henry's thinking on these issues is vividly on display in his 1963 *Aspects of Christian Social Ethics*. Originally delivered as part of Fuller Seminary's Payton Lectures, Henry here was at his best. The lectures, then collected and slightly expanded for publication, were never intended to be a comprehensive analysis of social ethics.[7] But his comments on economics are worth noting.

To begin with, Henry was quick to rehearse the inherent deficiencies of communism. But as he did so, he took particular aim at the ways in which the ideology had undercut social life from revealed truth for human flourishing.

In place of time-honored social forms validated by revealed religion, and still widely accepted as normative by society in general, Communism substitutes novel patterns of social life based on the totalitarian state, which takes control of family, of economic and political life, and of culture itself. Communist theory assails the *status quo* along lines that are anti-Christ

---

6 Howard E. Kershner, "Economic Facts and Fallacies" (speech delivered at the 1959 Pepperdine College Freedom Forum), Pepperdine College Freedom Forum Collection, Pepperdine University Libraries, https://pepperdine.contentdm. oclc.org/digital/collection/p15730coll19/id/422.

7 For more on Henry's contribution to evangelical ethics, see Richard Mouw, "Toward a Fully-Orbed Evangelical Ethic," in *Essential Evangelicalism: The Enduring Legacy of Carl F. H. Henry*, ed. Matthew Hall and Owen Strachan (Crossway, 2015), 43–58.

(that is, opposes Christian patterns of marriage, economics, and limited government) and anti-God (since it opposes the whole idea of supernaturally willed orders of responsibility.[8]

A Leninist sympathizer Henry was not. And yet, he also recognized that Marxist critiques of post-industrialist modern capitalism seemed to have growing resonance for understandable reasons. In particular, Henry was sympathetic to criticism of the ways in which automation and assembly line industrialization had resulted in a monotony of labor that had left workers unsure of their place. In his estimation, this was a challenge largely unmet by Protestant Christianity, which seemed to have little to say to the place of work in the Christian life in the early 1960s, leaving workers alienated from the vision of the kingdom of God and in turn creating an opening for Marxist critique:

> Communism seized the propaganda value of this sorry state of affairs by ascribing labor's feeling of frustration to the capitalist system. It proclaimed that capitalism inherently depreciates and exploits the working class. Promising instead a new world order that "glorifies" the worker, Communism soon quickened the lagging spirit of the laborer. If performed with thoroughgoing loyalty to "the Party" and with a view to the coming world revolution, even the most menial task now gained larger social significance. The worker thus joined a cause "wide as the world," one that promised the nobility and romance of personal recognition.[9]

But, Henry claimed, the system had not delivered on its promises: "The collectivist promise of status for the worker has become a tragic mirage.... The worker becomes merely a tool whose highest good is whole-souled subservience to the totalitarian state. Instead of being glorified, the worker is demeaned and degraded as a political mechanism."[10]

---

8 Carl F. H. Henry, *Aspects of Christian Social Ethics* (Eerdmans, 1964), 17.

9 Henry, *Aspects of Christian Social Ethics*, 34–35.

10 Henry, *Aspects of Christian Social Ethics*, 34–35.

In turn, Henry contended that working conditions of workers in capitalistic nations were measurably superior to those in communist economies. And while he did register concern about any form of assembly line work that would "destroy man's conviction of being a fellow-worker with God," Henry made clear that assembly line work was not evil *per se.* "Even monotony can be justified in the ministry of God and of humanity," he concluded, "if it stems from a constructive activity that has no better alternative."[11]

why not make a better

Concern Over Secular Communism *alternative* and Secular Capitalism

A new generation of evangelicals emerged in the late 1960s, many of them propelled in part by Henry's previous call for renewed social action. However, they were cynical of displays of patriotism and even skeptical that traditional American political and economic structures could be reconciled with biblical justice. Increasingly, they found themselves in an awkward dialogue with Henry.[12]

Some of this tension is apparent in a 1976 interview with Henry published in *Sojourners.* In his interview with the editors, including a young Jim Wallis, Henry exhibited his willingness to critique corruptions of capitalism.

> I think there are strengths to capitalism. But our failure to criticize capitalism, in its operation—the shoddy record of production for obsolescence, the reckless depletion of natural resources, the prizing of profit over sensitivity to worker's needs, the bribery by multi-national corporations, the big stake in smoking and cigarette production despite the fact that we know it to be harmful, the alcohol traffic—gave a one-way street to the Marxists to criticize capitalism, in such a way that our younger generation became enchanted with Marxism as an alternative.[13]

11 Henry, *Aspects of Christian Social Ethics*, 59.

12 For more on this movement, see David R. Swartz, *Moral Minority: The Evangelical Left in an Age of Conservatism* (University of Pennsylvania Press, 2012).

13 "Interview: Carl Henry on Evangelical Identity," *Sojourners*, April 1976, 32.

Decades later, Henry retained his willingness to defend capitalism against its critics while simultaneously denouncing its secular
forms.

> Capitalism is less than ideal economics when it lacks ecolog-
> ical responsibility and sensitivity for consumers, for labor, or
> for the jobless and the impoverished. In our fragile environ-
> ment insensitivity to human need encouraged indiscreet flir-
> tation with a bureaucratically controlled welfare state. Such
> possibilities do not automatically legitimate Marxist analysis
> and socialist economics. Socialist efforts to improve the state
> of the masses by redistributing wealth displayed little grasp of
> economics or of the complexity of the human condition; more
> and more one time champions of socialism now decry it as an
> abject failure. No Christian ought, however, to confuse the
> superiority of free enterprise as an economic system with the
> economics of the kingdom of God.[14]

In particular, Henry excoriated "establishment evangelicals" for
their failure "to criticize the American politico-cultural context,
including secular capitalism and seamy governmental trends." This
failure, he claimed, had actually served to weaken younger evangelicals' confidence in capitalist and free-market systems. "Uncrit-
ical commendation of the status quo," he concluded, "stimulated
hypercritical denunciation of it by the political left."[15]

Capitalism and Liberation in God,
Revelation, and Authority

Over the course of his six volumes, Henry sussed out more of his
thinking in *God, Revelation, and Authority*. In particular, Henry
devoted a surprising number of pages in volume four to the ris-
ing challenge of liberation theology. He sparred directly with the
thought of Gustavo Gutierrez and others, concluding that the

---

14 Carl F. H. Henry, *Gods of This Age or God of the Ages?* (Broadman & Holman, 1994), 41.

15 Carl F. H. Henry, *Evangelicals in Search of Identity* (Word, 1976), 70–71.

movement had shorn away anything resembling historic Christianity and had done so in particular by undermining the hermeneutical task itself. Indeed, he concluded that "Gutierrez is so one-sidedly concerned with political implications of the gospel—which he then expounds in an additionally one-sided way—that one wonders what his gospel truly is."[16]

Henry's concern was particularly centered on the destabilizing of an evangelical hermeneutic that privileged praxis above all else. In doing so, he cautioned that liberation theologies had swallowed a poison pill, one that inevitably led to any number of departures. As he put it, "Those who yield to Marx their little finger or right hand seem unaware that he wants nothing less than the whole man."[17] And yet, even here Henry maintained his caution against the ever-present temptation on the other extreme. He hoped evangelicals would find a better way, "one which refuses to baptize either Marxist socialism or secular capitalism as Christian."[18]

Henry cautioned against and avoided imposing modern capitalism on top of biblical hermeneutics, just as he excoriated Marxian alternatives: "All historical structures, whether capitalist, communist, socialist or any other, are equally under the searching judgment of the Christian revelation."[19] What was most urgent, Henry judged, was the threat of secularism to any enduring social ethic or morality: "Wherever secularism, especially secular capitalism, provides little or no moral stimulus, and readily accommodates and thrives on a spiritual vacuum, there Marxism exploits the realities of human discontent; it presents itself to the noncommunist world as a pristine humanism that imparts meaning and worth to individual life."[20]

In fact, Henry was even willing to critique "contemporary champions of capitalism" such as Hayek and Friedman, whom he faulted for exalting "freedom to an absolute in the context of libertarian principles that dwarf the question of proper limits."

16 Carl F. H. Henry, *God, Revelation and Authority*, vol. 4, *God Who Speaks and Shows* (Word, 1976), 560.

17 Henry, *God Who Speaks and Shows*, 586.

18 Henry, *God Who Speaks and Shows*, 560.

19 Henry, *God Who Speaks and Shows*, 587.

20 Henry, *God Who Speaks and Shows*, 585.

Similarly, while he appreciated Michael Novak's *The Spirit of Democratic Capitalism* for its persuasive arguments for capitalism's remarkable abilities, Henry noted disappointment that the book fell short of working "out the bearing of biblical ethics upon free market commitments."[21]

For his part, Henry concluded,

> Capitalism will thrive best in a society that is behaviorally aware of divine creation, providence and judgment. Yet free enterprise at least intrinsically incorporates certain economic values, notably a certain legitimacy of self-interest and the propriety of private property, even if these values, like others, can become idolatrous if taken out of a larger moral context.[22]

While some evangelicals—Henry noted Ron Sider and Richard Lovelace—called for economic redistribution in some form, Henry claimed that the Bible "ascribes economic injustice not to the possession of wealth but to its misuse. The God of Scripture judges his people because they do not recognize him as the ultimate source of their possessions, and because they do not use those possessions as responsible stewards."[23]

Global Evangelicalism and Social Action

Henry had long hoped for a pan-evangelical movement that would galvanize broad support not only in North America but far beyond. His role as chairman of the 1966 Berlin Congress on World Evangelization was one key milestone in that ambition. However, by the arrival of Lausanne Congress in 1974, some of that evangelical ambition seemed vulnerable to fracture and strain. Evangelicals largely agreed on the necessity of personal witness to the saving work of God in Christ as well as Christian social action in the world. But those twin commitments were often contested—and defined—in increasingly different ways.

---

21 Carl F. H. Henry, *God, Revelation and Authority*, vol. 6, *God Who Stands and Stays, Part Two* (Word, 1983), 476.

22 Henry, *God Who Stands and Stays*, 476.

23 Henry, *God Who Stands and Stays*, 474.

For his part, Henry arrived at Lausanne mindful of these shifts and seemed eager to speak to what he saw to be some of the most pressing issues. His address—"Christian Personal and Social Ethics in Relation to Racism, Poverty, War, and Other Problems"—attempted to propose some cohesive moral theory that could galvanize a consensus among the emerging global evangelical movement. In this context, Henry again reiterated the very real vulnerability to Marxist threats of confiscated wealth and forced redistribution. Among other factors, Henry indicted evangelicals whose "Christian proclamation speaks only of personal spiritual conversion, ignores social criticism attuned to biblical justice, and elaborates no persuasive alternative to forced redistribution of wealth either in theory or practice."[24] What was needed, he claimed, was for Christian critique to show that Marxist proposals could never overcome human alienation "but in fact perpetuate that alienation by substituting one preferred class for another and deepen it by ignoring man's fundamental spiritual relationships to the living God."[25]

Henry called for a renewed commitment to understandings of wealth, capital, property, and profit shaped by biblical revelation. In all of it, Henry reiterated his primary concern about the overarching threat of secularism. Christians needed to retain a theocentric vision of wealth, remembering that all they own is a matter of divine stewardship. As he put it, "No true Christian can be rich and use wealth merely for self-gratification."[26]

In particular, the question of the legitimacy of private property captured Henry's attention during this same period. For his part, Henry lamented the relative silence on the subject in most corners of Western societies. This neglect, he feared, created a vacuum for Communist criticisms of private property and rejections of its divine sanction. Here too, Henry grounded his social ethic of private property in the prior necessity of biblical revelation.

---

24 Henry, "Christian Personal and Social Ethics in Relation to Racism, Poverty, War, and Other Problems," in *Let the Earth Hear His Voice: International Congress on World Evangelization, Lausanne, Switzerland*, ed. J. D. Douglas (World Wide Publications, 1975), 1167.

25 Henry, "Christian Personal and Social Ethics," 1167–1168.

26 Henry, "Christian Personal and Social Ethics," 1173.

Like colonial rights to buy from Native Americas

"Any doctrine of property devoid of biblical legitimation will inevitably license immoral practices," he wrote. "When man as a sinful creature fashions and justifies the right of property in isolation from divine prerogatives, he no longer properly balances rights and responsibilities, but will compromise the one in protecting the other."[27] Henry's anxiety of an encroaching secularism was apparent in his assessment. While Marxist criticisms of the legitimacy of private property were self-apparent and brazen, he recognized that "secular capitalistic civilization" was untethered from any historic Judeo-Christian foundation that could adequately define the moral meaning of rights, responsibilities, and property. Accordingly, Henry contended that divine revelation was essential in defining and ordering private property. Christian theology thus had a "dual responsibility," to show "that the Communist rejection of private property misunderstands God's purpose for human society, and it must show that God's ordination of all things can be equally dimmed and distorted where human rights are promoted in a strictly secular manner."[28]

The New Right and Evangelical Identity in the 1980s

With the ascendancy of the New Right and the surging political power of the Religious Right, Henry found himself in an unexpected place. Others have reflected on his location within that story. But for our purposes, it is worth noting that Henry did not fundamentally shift in his engagement on these issues.

Some of Henry's peers took different paths. For example, Harold Lindsell even went so far as to publish his book *Free Enterprise: A Judeo-Christian Defense* in 1982. Lindsell claimed that the choice between the two options of socialism and capitalism was a rather obvious one. While "greed and human selfishness" would be present and universal realities until the eschaton, societies were faced with a decision necessarily informed by realism. Which of

---

27 Carl F. H. Henry, "Christian Perspective on Private Property," in *God and the Good: Essays in Honor of Henry Stob*, ed. Clifton Orlebeke and Lewis Smedes (Eerdmans, 1975), 95.

28 Henry, "Christian Perspective on Private Property," 99.

the two options "is more likely to prove beneficial to the greater number of people? In this regard, free enterprise is far and away the better economic system to contain human greed."[29] Lindsell would be joined by any number of evangelicals who would provide proof-text models, seemingly connecting chapter and verse to the contours of modern capitalism.

In an essay published in the *Christian Century* the day after Ronald Reagan's presidential victory, Henry was remarkably candid about some of his views and concerns. He noted, for example, that the modern world seemed gripped by increasingly "divergent" definitions of justice. He was reluctant for the nation to take on "even more staggering military expenditures." He speculated that

> inflation may now be irreversible, a specter spawned by political leaders whom we entrusted to watch the storehouse. It may also be that Western middle-class affluence will soon be recognized not as the universal ideal but as a remarkable exception in human history, one bearing great stewardship opportunities and responsibilities for worldwide extension of the gospel and for helping the underprivileged to help themselves.[30]

By this point in his life, a heightened sense of realism had settled in and Henry expressed skepticism that social activists could deliver more just or better structures. In his estimation, the people of God would have to await the eschaton and a new heavens and new earth. And yet, even here, Henry steered clear of the withdrawal he had always lamented within fundamentalism, especially the variety driven by premillennial dispensationalism: "To truncate the Christian mission simply to the changing of social structures profoundly misunderstands the biblical view of human nature and divine redemption. Yet we also truncate the gospel if we limit or circumvent that expectation that divine deliverance will extend 'as far as the curse is found.'"[31]

---

29 Harold Lindsell, *Free Enterprise: A Judeo-Christian Defense* (Tyndale House, 1982), 21.

30 Carl F. H. Henry, "Evangelicals in a Turning Time," *Christian Century*, 5 September 1980, 1061–1062.

31 Henry, "Evangelicals in a Turning Time," 1062.

For his part, Henry was measured and seemed conscious of the pitfalls on any number of sides. Writing in *The Christian Mindset in a Secular Society* (1984), Henry lamented the crass materialism of much of American culture and how it had undermined evangelicals' kingdom ethos: "One sure way to frustrate evangelical awakening is for Christians to effusively give Sunday to God but, for the rest of the week, to accommodate a secular lifestyle shaped by craven greed."[32]

As should be clear by now, this did not signal any erosion of his capitalist sympathies or rejection of Marxist models in all their forms. Henry was just as ardent as ever in his rejection of Marxist alternatives to American consumerism and greed:

> Free enterprise has immense values over against the bureaucratically controlled societies. I do not find in the Old Testament a single prophet or in the New Testament a single apostle who considers private property an evil; nor do I find the Christ of the Gospels equalizing the wealth either of the Jews or of the Romans of his day as the path to social or spiritual utopia. Stripped of moral answerability, however, free enterprise soon invites ethical censure by sensitive social critics and by ideologists given to socialist alternatives. More importantly, when free enterprise frees itself of God it invites the judgment of God.[33]

Just as he had in *Uneasy Conscience* nearly forty years before, Henry cautioned against a hollowed-out secular form of capitalism. If the inherent exploitation and corruptions of Marxism were apparent to all, Henry made clear that "secular capitalism is an ethically unbridled economic theory [that] likewise arouses the desire for material excess and indulgence."[34]

That same year, Henry pressed further on this core issue of secularism. In an address delivered in the spring of 1984, Henry took

---

32 Carl F. H. Henry, *The Christian Mindset in a Secular Society: Promoting Evangelical Renewal and National Righteousness* (Multnomah, 1984), 21.

33 Henry, *Christian Mindset in a Secular Society*, 22.

34 Henry, *Christian Mindset in a Secular Society*, 22.

aim at several fantasies of secular society, again confirming that his primary concern was the erosion of any Judeo-Christian ethical consensus. On the one hand, Henry cautioned against the illusion of presuming that capitalism could survive devoid of "moral and spiritual commitments."[35] Again, he warned of the threats posed by "secular capitalism" to Christian advance:

> Large corporations have frequently funded causes engaged in revolutionary social change. When big business promotes its products by trivializing for commercial purposes the spiritual and cultural heritage of the West (e.g., Baskin-Robbins's use of Handel's *Messiah* as background music to laud its "heavenly" ice cream), it indirectly weakens the Judeo-Christian inheritance. When the CBS network uses the "Hallelujah Chorus" to close out coverage of U.S. victories at the Pan-American Games, it not only betrays a lack of reverence but also serves to paganize the religious heritage of the West. The salvation God provides in Christ has nothing in common with athletic prowess. The use of Scripture references with a double entendre in cinema and theater frequently degrades into a crude joke, and sometimes into a carnal banter, what spiritually sensitive generations have prized as a sacred treasure.[36]

One cannot help but wonder what Henry would say if he were with us, witnessing the advent of Fortune 500 companies' role as handmaidens of a moral and sexual revolution.

However, Henry had not softened in his criticism of Marxist economic models. He still made clear that, while "the Bible teaches that God has a special eye for the destitute and that those who are entrusted with more than their needy neighbors have a duty to be compassionate," it "does not teach a forced redistribution of wealth."[37] Similarly, he rejected any charge that capitalism was to blame for poverty. Instead, Henry lamented the prevalence of a

---

35 Carl F. H. Henry, *Christian Countermoves in a Decadent Society* (Multnomah, 1986), 34.

36 Henry, *Christian Countermoves in a Decadent Society*, 34.

37 Henry, *Christian Countermoves in a Decadent Society*, 34.

far worse human poverty, one fostered by the "spiritual and moral rebellion of the human race." On this count, he contended that "the Marxist state" was guilty of compounding this deeper poverty by "suppression of public freedom."[38]

Henry maintained a cautious approach toward any theological instinct that would baptize an economic theory as distinctly Christian. Even more, he was leery of Christians who presumed that their own political, social, or economic context was to be normative. As he put it, "Whoever considers the politico-economic status quo sacred or normative, or uncritically resigns himself to it, needs to reread the Bible."[39]

By 1991, Henry was perhaps even more reflective. In an essay on the connections between the Bible and public policy, he noted how the old evangelical left of the 1970s—epitomized by Jim Wallis—had erred in their disavowal of capitalism. But he also noted the inherent problem with those, like Carl McIntyre, who had "defend[ed] capitalism as a natural outgrowth of biblical Christianity." Looking now to the 1990s and a post-Cold War era, Henry acknowledged that the apparent collapse of socialism may tempt some to "identify capitalism as Christian or biblical." That surely was understandable when even the socialists were beginning to suddenly warm up to markets. "Socialism seems to have been an artificially contrived collectivist theory, whereas free enterprise is compatible with the deepest human instincts. Yet to claim that capitalism is essentially Christian is to assimilate to Christianity an economic system capable of ethical indifference and injury."[40]

Henry surmised that God had providentially scattered the Church over two millennia in any number of varied political contexts and forms of government for a deliberate purpose, "in order to witness to the lordship of Jesus Christ as final judge of the nations." While evangelicals could not equate "democratic or republican political structures with the Kingdom of God," Henry

<hr>

38 Henry, *Christian Countermoves in a Decadent Society*, 34.

39 Carl F. H. Henry, "Biblical Authority and the Social Crisis," in *Authority and Interpretation: A Baptist Perspective*, ed. D. A. Garrett and R. R. Melick Jr. (Baker Books, 1987), 206.

40 Carl F. H. Henry, "Linking the Bible to Public Policy," in *Biblical Principles and Public Policy: The Practice*, ed. Richard C. Chewning (NavPress, 1991), 25.

surmised, "most nonetheless consider democratic government preferable in fallen history because of its promotion of political self-determination and the safeguards it offers against secular totalitarianism."[41]

In some of his most prescient evaluations, Henry proposed a more nuanced—even if still appreciative—assessment of capitalism.

> Is it more factual, then, simply to hold that free-market economics was superimposed on a religious outlook stressing voluntarism, hard work, and prudent management, and that the providential result was an unprecedented expansion in material production and wealth and in a remarkable improvement in the living standards of much of the citizenry? Shall we regard free enterprise as an ethically neutral system, or is it not rather the case that Christianity requires us to forgo the notion of value-free mechanisms? Given humanity's present fallen condition, capitalism is readily placed in the service of human inordinacy. While it is true that competition and the law restrict such inordinacy, does not mass media advertising create for shysters an unprecedented opportunity to disadvantage the consumer?[42]

In Henry's estimation, history had rendered its judgment, confirming that socialist systems were incapable of producing wealth. While evangelicals needed to be warned against succumbing to a flat hermeneutic that concluded that capitalism was the economy of the kingdom, Henry did affirm that it was an economic system compatible with the values of the kingdom. "Capitalism is not the economics of the Kingdom of God," Henry surmised, "but neither is it a grotesque ideology; it has openly exhibited its efficiency as a wealth-producing system, and biblical principles can prod it toward the ethical purposes that protect it from inordinate misuse." Henry's confidence in capitalism was resilient, insofar as free markets were informed by a Judeo-Christian moral tradition

---

41 Henry, "Linking the Bible to Public Policy," 22.
42 Henry, "Linking the Bible to Public Policy," 25.

Nobody listens in power

grounded in biblical revelation. He had little hope for a just society and economy animated by a crass secularism.

Conclusion

Writing later in life, Henry surveyed the transformations that had gripped the West by 1994. As he did, he seemed to revel in the significance of the moment, one in which modern capitalism seemed to have won the day and been vindicated against the backdrop of imploding global Communism and socialist economies in Europe:

> The liberals who were soft on communism or socialism have now had their day. Soviet dominion over Eastern Europe has ended—the Soviet Union has itself collapsed. The historical momentum is clearly toward democratic self-determination, free enterprise, and private property. Those who considered socialism the wave of the future—especially liberation theologians who taught that God keeps a socialist eye on the poor— are now exposed as deluded ideologues.[43]

Francis Fukuyama's "The End of History" it was not, but Henry's conclusions here were replicated throughout the West in general and within American evangelicalism in particular.[44]

A few concluding thoughts are in order. First, Henry may offer to evangelical theologians in our time a healthy model for careful engagement on any number of issues of public policy, including economics. While Henry did not shy away from addressing these issues, he retained sufficient epistemic humility to recognize he was *not* a trained economist. Our generation seems to be one that demands that so-called "thought leaders" have something to say on every matter and the hotter the hot take the better (at least for clicks and likes). But perhaps there is a better way.

Second, Henry's call to prioritize the redemptive essence of biblical Christianity seems more timely than ever. Evangelicals

---

43 Henry, *Gods of This Age?*, 18.

44 Francis Fukuyama, *The End of History and the Last Man* (New York: Free Press, 1992).

are never far from re-enacting the mistakes of past generations, no matter our chronological snobbery. While some are tempted by the allure of some sort of Protestant appropriation of Catholic integralism or even a resurgent theonomy and reconstructionism, Henry gives us a better path. While those voices would likely agree with Henry's diagnosis of the social cost of an eroding cultural Christianity under the corrosive acids of secularity, they offer a poison pill, one that confuses the ontological realities of the Kingdom of God and the anticipation of the people of God for the eschatalogical fulfillment of our deepest longings. As Henry put it, "In a fallen world, utopia must wait for the Lord's return."[45]

---

45 Henry, "Linking the Bible to Public Policy," 28.

8

Cocoa for Cloth: The Use of "Our Lands, Goods, and Bodies" in the Life of William Kiffen

Michael A.G. Haykin

UNLIKE OTHER CHRISTIAN TRADITIONS, the Particular Baptists do not point back to one key individual theologian as their founder. Instead, their name recalls the rediscovery of certain elements of a vital New Testament ordinance. Thus, when the Particular Baptists emerged in the seventeenth century from the womb of English Puritanism during the British Civil Wars (1638–1651) and established their theological boundaries in what has come to be called the *First London Confession of Faith* (1644/1646), they insisted that only believers undergo baptism and that it be done by immersion. Most of the main authors who defended this conviction in that world have been long forgotten. Ironically, the two seventeenth-century figures that many recall as Baptist pioneers, Roger Williams (c.1603–1684) and John Bunyan (1628–1688), were actually not in the mainstream of Baptist life: Williams was a committed Baptist less than a year while Bunyan did not think that believer's baptism was necessary for entry into a Christian community.

If there is one truly central figure in the emergence of the British Particular Baptist movement in this era, it would have to be William Kiffen (1616–1701). When Joseph Ivimey (1773–1834), the nineteenth-century Baptist historian, published a biography of Kiffen in 1833, he did so in the conviction that the seventeenth-century Particular Baptist leader was "one of the most extraordinary persons whom the [Particular Baptist] denomination has produced, both as to the consistency and correctness of his principles and the eminence of his worldly and religious character."

Ivimey especially hoped that his account of Kiffen's life and ministry would spur his younger Baptist contemporaries to take Kiffen
as "a pattern of piety and integrity."[1] To what degree this hope was
realized cannot be pursued here. What this paper does seek to explore is the way that Kiffen sought to use material wealth in his life
as an expression of Christian discipleship. Kiffen often used his
wealth to further what he saw to be the Christian cause of his day,
and despite being accused of forgetting his more modest roots,
Kiffen never lost sight of his duty to provide for the poor under
his care. Modern Christians of significant means would do well to
follow his lead.

"Them they called Puritan ministers"

By seventeenth-century standards, as shall be seen, Kiffen was fab-
ulously wealthy. This was highly unusual, since Kiffen was also a
Particular Baptist pastor for some sixty years in the heart of London. Most of his fellow pastors and fellow Baptists were drawn from
either the poor or the lower strata of the middle class—cloth-work-
ers, artisans, and tradesmen. Thus Benjamin Keach (1640–1704)
and Hercules Collins (1646/7–1702) were both tailors by training; John Spilsbury (1593–c.1662/68) a cobbler; Thomas De-
laune (c.1635/45–1685) a schoolmaster; and Andrew Gifford,
Sr. (1641–1721), a cooper. Even Kiffen's close colleague Hanserd
Knollys (1599–1691), who was Cambridge-educated and an Anglican minister before he joined the ranks of the Particular Baptists,
was called to pastor an impoverished London congregation and
became poor as a result.[2] Kiffen himself, when he entered his teens,
was apprenticed most likely to a glover. There seems to be no truth
in the common assertion that he served as an apprentice to John
Lilburne (1614–1657), well known to history as an agitator for the

---

1 Joseph Ivimey, *The Life of Mr. William Kiffin* (London, 1833), xi, ii. This
work is an annotated and edited version of Kiffen's autobiography. For the spelling of Kiffen's name, I am following the leading authority on the life and ministry of Kiffin, namely, Larry Kreitzer of Regent's Park College, Oxford University.

2 William Kiffen, "The Epistle to the Reader," in *The Life and Death of That
Old Disciple of Jesus Christ, and Eminent Minister of the Gospel, Mr. Hanserd
Knollys* (John Harris, 1692), A3 recto.

social radicalism of the Levellers, who had a completely egalitarian vision of society, though Kiffen and Lilburne were friends in later years.[3]

In 1631, depressed about his future prospects as a glover, he decided to run away from his master. Providentially, he happened to go by St. Antholin's Church, where the Puritan Thomas Foxley (fl. 1640) was preaching that day on the fifth commandment and happened to illustrate it with "the duty of servants to masters." Seeing a crowd of people going into the church, Kiffen decided to join them. As has been the experience of many under the Spirit-anointed preaching of the Word, Kiffen was convinced that Foxley's sermon was intentionally directed at him. He decided to go back to his master with the resolve to hear regularly "some of them they called Puritan ministers."[4]

"That order laid down by Christ and his apostles"

During the 1630s, however, the Puritans, the radical element within the Church of England, came under extreme pressure to bring their thinking and behavior into line with the views of William Laud (1573–1645), who had become Archbishop of Canterbury in 1633. Laud was strongly Arminian in his theology, as well as being firmly convinced that the ritual of the Church of England—such things as the wearing of vestments by ministers, the orientation and ornamentation of the communion table, and the use of the sign of the cross in the baptismal service—had the full approval of God. He sought to impose such uniformity of ritual and doctrine in the Church of England and refused to make any allowance for the individual conscience. Rather than conform, a goodly number of individuals left England either for the Netherlands or for

---

3 For a helpful overview of the Levellers and their ideas, see Andrew Bradstock, *Radical Religion in Cromwell's England: A Concise History from the English Civil War to the End of the Commonwealth* (I. B. Tauris, 2011), 27–50. See William Kiffen, preface to *The Christian mans triall: or, A true relation of the first apprehension and severall examinations of John Lilburne*, 2nd ed. (William Larnar, 1641).

4 William Orme, *Remarkable Passages in the Life of William Kiffin* (Burton and Smith, 1823), 3.

New England. Others, though, refused to quit their homeland and
formed or joined what the Church of England regarded as illegal
conventicles. Amongst the latter was Kiffen.

By 1638 Kiffen had come to reject Anglican arguments for the
idea of a state church and had joined what he once termed "a company of saints in a congregational way" in London.[5] Two years later, Kiffen accepted an invitation to preach to the congregation, later known as Devonshire Square Baptist Church, and at some point
over the course of the next three or four years, Kiffen was chosen
as their pastor. During this entire period, Kiffen continued to study
the Bible for direction with regard to the constitution and form of
a local church. When, over forty years later, he recalled this period
of his life, what stuck out in his memory was his diligent examination of the Bible to find the "right way of worship,"[6] which entailed
discovering *the* ecclesial blueprint embedded in the New Testament. By the fall of 1642, he and his congregation had arrived at
what they believed to be such a blueprint, namely, what would later be described as a Baptist church. As he wrote about this search
in these years in his *A Sober Discourse of Right to Church-Communion* (1681):

> After some time [I] concluded that the safest way was to fol-
> low the footsteps of the flock (namely that order laid down by
> Christ and his apostles, and practiced by the primitive Chris-
> tians in their times) which I found to be that after conversion
> they were baptized, added to the church, and continued in the
> apostles' doctrine, fellowship, breaking of bread, and prayer;
> according to which I thought myself bound to be conformable.[7]

---

5 William Kiffen, "The Epistle to the Christian Reader," *in A Glimpse of Sions
Glory: or The Churches' Beautie specified* (William Larnar, 1641). See Orme, *Remarkable Passages*, 14.

6 William Kiffen, "To the Christian Reader," in *A Sober Discourse of Right to
Church-Communion* (Enoch Prosser, 1681), A2 recto. In subsequent quotations
from Kiffen's writings, the capitalization and spelling has been modernized.

7 Kiffen, "To the Christian Reader," A2 recto–A2 verso. His commitment to
the Calvinistic Baptist cause appears to have been sealed by a public debate with
the Anglican apologist Daniel Featley (1582–1645) that was held on October 17,
1642, in Southwark.

"Our lands, goods, and bodies"

Two years later he was a signatory for his church, along with the leadership of six other London congregations, of *The First London Confession of Faith* (1644). Kiffen not only signed this document but also appears to have played a significant role in drafting it along with John Spilsbury and another Particular Baptist pastor, Samuel Richardson (fl. 1637–1658). This confession demonstrated the solidarity of the Particular Baptists with the Reformed community throughout Europe as well as spelling out in detail a Baptist ecclesiology. It also served as the theological basis for the Particular Baptists during their rapid advance throughout the British Isles and Ireland in the late 1640s and the 1650s—the confession was reprinted a number of times during this period—and then throughout the years of persecution in the 1660s and 1670s after the Restoration of the monarchy. It would only be replaced at the dawn of the long eighteenth century by the *Second London Confession of Faith* (1677/1688).

This confession also responded to various scurrilous accusations that had been made against the Particular Baptists, one of which was that they were subversive revolutionaries like some of the Anabaptists of the previous century. The lie to this accusation was given in five articles at the close of the confession, in which, among other things, Kiffen and his co-authors acknowledged the necessity of being obedient to governing authorities, using "our lands, goods, and bodies" in such a way as to demonstrate obedience "in the Lord" to them. Kiffen, Spilsbury, and Richardson were convinced that the Scriptures called upon them as Baptists to defend with force both these authorities and "all civil laws made by them, with our persons, liberties, and estates, with all that is called ours."[8] In other words, Christian piety encompassed both one's relationship to lawful authorities as well as the way that one used one's "lands, goods, and bodies."

Now Kiffen and his friends crafted this confessional text in the midst of the early stages of the British Civil Wars. But despite the

---

8 *The First London Confession of Faith* (1644) LII, XLIX, in *Baptist Confessions of Faith*, ed. William L. Lumpkin, rev. ed. (Judson, 1969), 170, 169.

religious and political upheaval caused by these wars, Kiffen flourished as a merchant. He had joined the Worshipful Company of the
Leathersellers of London in 1638, which had enjoyed a monopoly
on the leather trade in the capital since the late Middle Ages. A decision around 1645 to take a member of his church as a partner for
a trading venture in Holland turned out to be the launching of an
enormously successful business. In his own words, "it pleased God
so to bless our endeavors, that, from scores of pounds, he brought
it to many hundreds and thousands of pounds: giving me more of
this world than ever I could have thought to have enjoyed."[9] In later years, it would appear that the focus of Kiffen's ventures was the
cloth trade.

Kiffen's successful business ventures also led to involvement in
the civic and political affairs of the capital. In 1642, along with other individual Londoners, Kiffen contributed horses and riders for
the Parliamentary cause. Documents from the late 1650s speak of
Kiffen as a "captain" and then "lieutenant-colonel" in the London
militia.[10] And in one noteworthy instance, Kiffen was called upon
to help in the international affairs of Cromwell's government. In
1655 and 1656, Cromwell was seeking to forge a Protestant alli-
ance with Sweden against the Papacy and the kingdom of Spain,
who were engaged in the active persecution of Protestants in such
places as northern Italy. It was decided that one or two substantial
gifts were to be given to the Swedish ambassador Christer Bonde
as a token of Cromwell's respect for the Swedish government. Kiff-
en was asked to supply a bolt of cloth, either one of silk or one
embroidered with gold or silver thread. Kiffen secured a bolt of
white silk cloth worth some £1200. In today's currency, this would
be around £185,000. What is staggering is that Kiffen could have
easily given this as a gift, but Cromwell insisted on repaying him
with money from the sale of a massive supply of cocoanuts that the
Cromwellian government had acquired from Jamaica.[11] With the
restoration of the monarchy in 1660, Kiffen's involvement in polit-

---

9 Orme, *Remarkable Passages*, 23.

10 *Discourse Between Cap. Kiffen, and Dr. Chamberlain*; *Life and Approaching Death of William Kiffen*, 5.

11 See Larry J. Kreitzer, "Using Chocolate to Pay for Silk—William Kiffen
and the Gift of Cloth for the Swedish Ambassador in 1656," in *William Kiffen and*

ical and civic matters understandably became curtailed, but Kiffen continued to use his wealth for good.

In 1664, for instance, he was able to rescue twelve General Baptists from Aylesbury, Buckinghamshire, who had been sentenced to death under an old Elizabethan law for participation in an illegal conventicle. When Kiffen was informed of the plight of these individuals, he went directly to Charles II (1630–1685), the king who had been restored to the monarchy in 1660, and obtained from him a reprieve for all of them.[12] The following decade, he also used his influence at court to clear some New England Baptists from the false charge of murdering a Boston minister. A quaint account of Kiffen's influential relationship with the king is found in a story related by the eighteenth-century Baptist historian Thomas Crosby (1683–1751).[13] The king had supposedly asked Kiffen for a loan of £40,000. Kiffen was aware that if he gave the king such a loan there was every likelihood that it would never be repaid. He thus offered to make the king a gift of £10,000, which the king gladly accepted. Afterward, according to Crosby, Kiffen jocosely remarked that he had thereby saved himself £30,000! This story may well be an inflated recollection of an incident in the summer of 1670 when a financially-burdened monarch approached the magistracy of London for a loan of £60,000. The response on the part of the aldermen was half-hearted. They raised but a third of the needed loan. Seeing an opportunity to drive a wedge between the king and parliament, London Dissenters organized the raising of the other two-thirds of the requested loan. Kiffen, who subscribed £3,600, was the largest of the contributors.

"The hand of God in all our sorrows"

In the 1670s and the early 1680s, Kiffen was embroiled in a controversy with the quintessential Puritan, John Bunyan, over the necessity of believer's baptism. Bunyan's *A Confession of my Faith, and A Reason of my Practice* (1672) and *Differences in Judgment About*

---

his World (Part 3), Re-Sourcing Baptist History: Seventeenth Century 3 (Centre for Baptist History and Heritage, Regent's Park College, 2013), 256–275.

12 Orme, *Remarkable Passages*, 117–120.

13 Thomas Crosby, *The History of the English Baptists* (London, 1740), III, 4.

Water-Baptism, No Bar to Communion (1673) had rejected the standard Particular Baptist argument that believer's baptism must precede membership in the local church or any of the privileges of that membership, in particular, participation in the Lord's Supper. While there were other written responses to Bunyan, it is Kiffen's *A Sober Discourse of Right to Church-Communion* (1681), characterized by "clear logic and crisp presentation,"[14] which serves as the most noteworthy advocacy of the closed membership position in this controversy. Although Bunyan is currently one of the most celebrated Christian authors of the seventeenth century, in his own day, he had little influence amongst his fellow Baptists since his strong commitment to open communion and open membership put him out of step with most seventeenth-century Particular Baptists, who, like Kiffen, were committed to closed communion and closed membership.[15] What is ironic about this controversy is that Bunyan, who had been a tinker, a mender of pots and pans, before his call to preach, accused Kiffen of slighting his social origins. Had Kiffen's enormous wealth led him to forget his own humble origins?

The years following the publication of this major work by Kiffen were difficult ones for him personally. His wife Hanna, whom he had married in 1638, died on October 6, 1682. Their two eldest sons had predeceased her: William (1649–1669), the eldest, had died at the age of twenty at the close of August, 1669, and another son had died in Venice, whom Kiffen was convinced had been poisoned by a Roman Catholic priest. A daughter, Priscilla (1655–1679), had also predeceased Hanna Kiffin; she died in March of 1679 at the age of twenty-four.

---

14 T. L. Underwood, "'It pleased me much to contend': John Bunyan as Controversialist," *Church History* 57, no. 4 (December 1988): 468.

15 On the controverted question about whether or not Bunyan actually was a Baptist, see Thomas Armitage, *A History of the Baptists* (Bryan, Taylor, & Co., 1887), 529–539; John Brown, *John Bunyan (1628–1688): His Life, Times, and Work*, rev. Frank Mott Harrison (Hulbert, 1928), 221–225, 236–238; Joseph D. Ban, "Was John Bunyan a Baptist? A Case-Study in Historiography," *Baptist Quarterly* 30, no. 8 (October 1984): 367–376. I would agree with the estimation of Richard L. Greaves when he states that "Bunyan is rightly regarded as an open-membership Baptist." Richard L. Greaves, "Conscience, Liberty, and the Spirit: Bunyan and Nonconformity," in *John Bunyan: Conventicle and Parnassus: Tercentenary Essays*, ed. N. H. Keeble (Clarendon, 1988), 35.

One of the sharpest blows was yet to come, though—what Kiffen called "no small affliction."[16] Upon the death of Charles II in 1685, his brother, the Roman Catholic James II (1633–1701), succeeded to the throne. A good number of people, though, regarded James Scott (1649–1685), the 1st Duke of Monmouth, a professing Protestant and the eldest illegitimate son of Charles II, as the rightful heir. A rebellion was fomented in the Monmouth's favor during the summer of 1685, but it was eventually crushed by James at the Battle of Sedgemoor (1685) with much bloodshed. Among those who had supported the Duke's bid for power were two of Kiffen's grandsons, William and Benjamin Hewling.

Both were apprehended after the failure of the rebellion, tried, and executed in September of 1685—William at Lyme Regis in Dorset on September 12, Benjamin at Taunton in Somerset on September 30. Kiffen unsuccessfully sought to obtain their freedom by offering £3,000—some £465,000 in today's currency—for their acquittal.[17] At the sentencing of William Hewling, the judge, George Jeffreys (1645–1689) publicly told him, "You have a grandfather who deserves to be hanged as richly as you."[18] Kiffen later had the opportunity to tell James II that the deaths of his two grandsons were "a wound to my heart, which ... never will close, but in the grave."[19] Within three years of Monmouth's rebellion, James's regime crumbled in the Glorious Revolution of 1688 when James II's son-in-law, the Dutch prince William of Orange (1650–1702), staged a coup d'état. The following year, William (now William III) authorized the Act of Toleration that gave the Dissenters religious freedom.

Kiffen, along with other Baptist leaders in London, employed the freedom of this new era to issue a call in July of 1689 for a national assembly of Calvinistic Baptists, the first of its kind. Representatives from over one hundred churches gathered. Amongst other things, they approved the adoption of the *Second London Confession of Faith*, originally drawn up in 1677 by William Collins

---

16 Orme, *Remarkable Passages*, 54.

17 Orme, *Remarkable Passages*, 54.

18 T. B. Macaulay, *The History of England from the Accession of James II* (repr., E. H. Butler, 1849), I, 436.

19 Orme, *Remarkable Passages*, 159.

and Nehemiah Coxe. This confession has been rightly described as "the most influential and important of all Baptist Confessions."[20] And the second name on the list of those who gave their formal approval to it was that of Kiffen, who signed for the church that he pastored at Devonshire Square in London.

Coda

Near the beginning of his career as a Particular Baptist, Kiffen had had occasion to write a small preface for an anonymous tract entitled *A Glimpse of Zion's Glory: or The Churches' Beauty Specified*. It contained one of his strongest statements about his commitment to congregationalism:

> Christian reader, thou hast here presented to thy view a small tract: the matter whereof is weighty, and of concernment to all that are the professed subjects of Jesus Christ. It is a thing of sad consequence to consider how we have been kept under blindness and darkness, although not totally, yet in great measure, in regard of such truths as do immediately strike at Antichrist and his false power. As namely this great truth, Christ the King of his church; and that Christ hath given this power to his church, not to a hierarchy, neither to a national presbytery, but to a company of saints in a congregational way.[21]

Nearly fifty years later when he signed the *Second London Confession of Faith*, his view regarding the nature of church governance had not changed. He was now an extremely wealthy man, as we have seen. Yet, he was still convinced, as he had been in the early 1640s that it was to the mostly poor members of his church that God had committed its governance—"a company of saints in a congregational way" and that the wealth that he had been given was to be employed for the good of such saints.

---

20 W. J. McGlothlin, *Baptist Confessions of Faith* (American Baptist Publication Society, 1911), 219.

21 William Kiffen, "The Epistle to the Christian Reader," in *A Glimpse of Zion's Glory: or The Churches' Beauty Specified* (William Larnar, 1641).

9

"Something Divine Mingled among Them": Care for the Parentless and the Poor as Ecclesial Apologetic in the Second Century

Timothy Paul Jones

APOLOGETICS is in crisis.

Apologetics may even be approaching its demise—or at least that's what the title of one recent text seemed to suggest.

The End of Apologetics were the words that greeted me from the front cover of this book. The title probably should have concerned me more than it did. The end of apologetics could seriously complicate my life, after all, since my livelihood depends in part on this discipline for which graveside services are apparently being planned.

As I read this work from philosopher and pastor Myron Bradley Penner, I was relieved to learn that it's not the entirety of apologetics that is headed down the same driveway as the dodo and the diplodocus. It is only—in Penner's words—"the Enlightenment project of attempting to establish a rational foundation for Christian belief" that is dying.[1] Apparently the more appropriate title—*The End of Establishing a Rational Foundation for Christianity after the Enlightenment*—had failed to warm the hearts of the publisher's marketing team.

According to Penner, no rational common ground remains today on which the Christian and the non-Christian can meet. To seek any rational common ground is to grant that ground to secularity. As a result, apologetics that attempts to mount an argument from any shared rational foundation could be, according to this book, "the single biggest threat to genuine Christian

---

1 Myron Penner, *The End of Apologetics: Christian Witness in a Postmodern Context* (Baker Academic, 2013), 7.

faith that we face today."[2]

The use of rational arguments is "a kind of violence," Penner says, that rips a person's cognitive commitments out of the larger context of his or her life.[3] Christians cannot correct this crisis simply by using rational arguments within the larger context of a relationship with an unbeliever. The arguments themselves *are* the problem in a postmodern age because the very notion of a common rational foundation is no longer true and because such arguments reduce a person to his or her status of rational belief or unbelief. If postmodern apologetics are properly done, rational apologetics and postmodern apologetics are mutually exclusive. When an apologist attempts to use a rational argument to convince someone to become a follower of Jesus, the rational form of the apologetic contradicts the relational content of the message.[4] *The End of Apologetics* sees rational apologetics as an approach that is not embodied in a community, that reduces listeners to their rational commitments, and that unnecessarily separates form and content.

The alternative is a uniquely postmodern witness in which the content becomes indistinguishable from the form.[5] A Christian who witnesses in this way declares to the world, "This is the truth I have encountered that has edified me. Take a look at my life, who I am and see if you think that it's true. And I believe that if you consider your own life and appropriate this truth, you will find it edifying for you too." Such a witness requires not only an individual but also a community "in which truthful speech is made evident

---

2 Penner, *The End of Apologetics*, 12; see also 183.

3 Penner, *The End of Apologetics*, 150, 161.

4 Others have rightly pointed out that presuppositional apologists have raised similar critiques for decades regarding the function of rational arguments in classical and evidential apologetics, albeit with different solutions. It is perplexing that no engagement with these critiques or alternate solutions appears anywhere in *The End of Apologetics*. See Nate Claiborne, "The End of Apologetics," Gospel Coalition, 15 August 2014, https://www.thegospelcoalition.org/reviews/end-apologetics.

5 Penner, *The End of Apologetics*, 90. In the end, what is intended by the phrase "the end of apologetics" on the cover of this book seems to include not only the demise of modern apologetics but also a rethinking of the goal—the "end" in the sense of the *telos*—of apologetics.

by the quality and character of their practices and life together."[6] The church's living testimony to the way of the cross reveals the deficiencies in the way of the world.

What I wish to challenge in this context is not the critique of rational apologetics in *The End of Apologetics* but the post-epistemological solution that the book presents as the most effective form of witness in a secular age. In Penner's model, the evidence that is recognizable and accessible to those outside of Christ in a secular context seems to be limited to the work of the Word in the lives and conversations of Christians. This evidence, while certainly not unimportant, leaves little place for history, reason, defenses of Holy Scripture, or arguments from the order of the cosmos— each one of which has, in different times and ways, characterized the church's apologetics long before the Enlightenment was ever a gleam in any philosopher's eye. In an attempt to reject the types of rational apologetics that succeeded the Enlightenment, *The End of Apologetics* ends up abandoning vast tracts of the Christian tradition that flourished prior to the Enlightenment.

The Exit Door You're Looking for May Be behind You

All of which brings us to a premodern alternative that *The End of Apologetics* leaves unconsidered.

The End of Apologetics seems to brush aside any possibility of a premodern solution by merely mentioning that "the material connections that gave rise to modernity testify to the inability of premodern views of the world to sustain themselves."[7] This casual dismissal of *a premodern view of the world* fails, however, to negate the possibility that *some patterns from the premodern church's witness in hostile cultural contexts might still provide a solution* that counteracts the dilemmas raised by the conditions of secularity.

With that in mind, I wish to suggest a possibility for apologetics that's repeated thousands of times each day on airport runways during pre-flight safety briefings: "Remember, the exit door you're looking for could be behind you." The escape from the problems

---

6 Penner, *The End of Apologetics*, 103–104, 127–128, 139.

7 Penner, *The End of Apologetics,* 13 n. 30.

pointed out in *The End of Apologetics* may not be in front of us in the form of a postmodern apologetic but behind us in the earliest Christian centuries.

In the second century in particular, a multiplicity of Christian writers—including Aristides of Athens, Athenagoras of Athens, Justin, and the author of *Epistle to Diognetus,* to name a few—grounded key portions of their arguments in the embodied ethics of the Christian community. For these second-century apologists, the moral habits of the church provided common ground on which to structure their arguments. This common ground was not "common" in the sense that Christians and non-Christians both practiced these ethics or even in the sense that both aspired to practice these ethics. Christian ethics provided a common ground in the sense that even non-Christians could not deny that this was how Christians lived. This argument did not require agreement on the terms of a rational common ground; it required the common recognition of a particular pattern of life.

For the Christians who articulated this apologetic, the life of the church was not merely *a context for the practice of Christian faith* but *a primary evidence for the truth of Christian faith.* To put it another way, their apologetic was, at least in part, *an ecclesial apologetic*—an argument that contended for the truth that the church confesses on the basis of the life that the church lives. The moral habits that sustained ecclesial apologetics in the ancient church encompassed a wide range of countercultural practices, including sexual continence, truthfulness, justice, contentment, kindness, humility, and honor for parents.[8] The focus of this research, however, is on a single strand within these ethics that was particularly prominent among the church's moral habits—sacrificial care for orphans and for the poor. A close examination of this moral habit in the second century reveals an ecclesial apologetic that was grounded in the Spirit-empowered work of the people of God on behalf of the vulnerable. What I intend to show in this research is how the early church's care for the parentless and the

---

8 See, e.g., Aristides of Athens, *Apol.* 15. For the text of Aristides's *Apology,* see Aristides, *Apologie,* ed. Bernard Pouderon and Marie-Joseph Pierre, SC 470 (Sources chrétiennes, 2003).

poor functioned as an ecclesial apologetic, testifying to the truthfulness and orthodoxy of the church's confession on the basis of the church's moral habits.

1. *"Something Divine Mingled among Them"*: Generosity to the Vulnerable and the Necessity of a Divine Presence in the Church in the Apology of Aristides

"Aristides," Eusebius of Caesarea wrote in the fourth century, "has left to posterity a defense of the faith."[9] Despite the preservation of this defense "by a great number" of Christians in the time of Eusebius, the *Apology* of Aristides was thought for several centuries to be lost. Those assumptions began to crumble in 1878, when a group of monastic scholars in Venice published a Latin translation of an Armenian rendering of the text. A Syriac translation of the *Apology* emerged a few years later. At that point, it became clear that the *Apology* had never been completely lost at all. Centuries earlier, portions of a Greek text of the *Apology* had been separated, reworked, and incorporated into a Christian novel known as *Barlaam and Ioasaph*.

Thus the text of this *Apology* does not survive in a single edition but in variant recensions, scattered across three fourth-century Greek fragments, a Syriac translation, an Armenian translation, and an eleventh-century novel that preserves portions of the text in Greek.[10] Although surviving versions of the *Apology* include a number of expansions and interpolations, the sections that form the focus for this particular research are not incongruent with a text written in the second century.[11]

---

9 Eusebius of Caesarea, *Ecclesiastical History*, vol. 5, *Books 1–5*, trans. Kirsopp Lake, LCL 153 (Harvard University Press, 1926), 4.3.3.

10 Markus Vinzent, *Writing the History of Early Christianity: From Reception to Retrospection* (Cambridge University Press, 2019) 206. For textual sources, see the modified stemma in William Rutherford, "Reinscribing the Jews: The Story of Aristides' *Apology* 2.2–4 and 14.1b–15.2," *HTR* 106, no. 1 (January 2013): 66.

11 Although the particular sections in *Apology* that focus on care for orphans, widows, and the poor are not incongruent with a second-century origin, the text of the *Apology* of Aristides cannot be established with certainty prior to fourth century on the basis of the extant manuscripts; it is not inconceivable that

Aristides addressed his *Apology* to one of two Roman emperors, Hadrian and Antoninus Pius, or perhaps both of them, depending on which version of the *Apology* represents the initial text. Regardless of which emperor Aristides named as the addressee, it seems unlikely that any emperor actually read this work.[12]

Aristides of Athens begins his defense by appealing to the beauty of creation and then to an argument from motion that seems to parallel a portion of Aristotle's *Metaphysics*:[13]

> When I had considered the sky and the earth and the seas and had surveyed the sun and the rest of creation, I marveled at the beauty. I perceived the world and all that is therein are moved by the power of another: God who is hidden in them and veiled by them. (*Apol.* 1)

Although Aristides appeals to a line of reasoning that later apologists would classify under the heading of classical arguments, his usage of these arguments is intended more to raise a question than to provide an answer. His goal is not to demonstrate the existence of a generic deity; it is to declare the inexplicability of the cosmos apart from a sovereign deity and then to define what attributes would need to characterize such a deity. According to Aristides, the cosmos requires a deity who is "immortal, perfect, and incomprehensible" (*Apol,* 1), and this brings Aristides to the undergirding

---

expansions of the text took place during and prior to the fourth century. See William Simpson, "Aristides' *Apology* and the Novel *Barlaam and Ioasaph*" (PhD diss., King's College London, 2015), 238–239.

12 Apologies may have been intended less to convert the unconverted and more to create a strong group identity among Christians. See Loveday Alexander, "The Acts of the Apostles as an Apologetic Text," in *Apologetics in the Roman Empire: Pagans, Jews, and Christians,* ed. Mark Edwards (Oxford University Press, 1999), 19; Tessa Rajak, "Talking at Trypho: Christian Apologetics as Anti-Judaism in Justin's Dialogue with Trypho the Jew," in Edwards, *Apologetics in the Roman Empire,* 25.

13 Aristotle, "Ἀριστοτέλους τῶν Μετά τα Φυσικά Λ," in *Metaphysics,* vol. 2, *Books 10–14. Oeconomica. Magna Moralia,* trans. Hugh Tredennick and G. Cyril Armstrong, LCL 287 (Harvard University Press, 1935), 12:6–9 (1071b). See Thomas Gaston, "The Influence of Platonism on the Early Apologists," *HeyJ* (2009): 577.

dilemma on which he structures the bulk of his argument: *Which of the four types of people in the world—barbarians, Greeks, Jews, or Christians—serves a deity that meets these requirements, and what manner of life does the worship of each of type of people produce?*

Aristides concludes that "Christians, as we have learned from their writings, have come closer to the truth and genuine knowledge than the rest" (*Apol.* 15)—but this is only the starting point for Aristides's positive argument for Christianity. It is the question of what "manner of life" Christianity produces that remains most relevant for the purposes of this research. It is at this point that Aristides begins to develop a clear ecclesial apologetic that defends the truthfulness of Christianity on the basis of the church's way of life.

After pointing to the church's ethics of sexual continence, kindness, honesty, and rejection of idolatry, Aristides turns his focus toward the care of Christians for the vulnerable and the poor:

> They do not turn away their respect from widows, and they redeem the orphan from the one who abuses him. Those who have give without boasting to the one who has not. When they see a stranger, they take him into their homes and rejoice over him like a brother; for they call each other brothers, not after the flesh but after the spirit, in God. Whenever one of their poor passes from the world, each one according to his ability pays attention and carefully sees to his burial. If they hear that one of their number is imprisoned or afflicted on account of the name of their Messiah, all of them eagerly minister to his necessity, and if it is possible to redeem the imprisoned one, they set him free. If there is anyone among them who is poor and needy and they have no spare food, they fast two or three days in order to supply the needy in their lack of food.... They do not proclaim the kind deeds that they do in the ears of the crowd, but they are careful that no one should notice them; they conceal their giving like one who finds a treasure and conceals it. (*Apol.* 15)

These habits of life are an integral part of the argument that drives Aristides to deliver some of the most memorable lines in his

Apology. "Truly," Aristides declares, "this is a new people, and there is something divine mingled among them" (*Apol.* 16). The life of the church is, for Aristides, a confirmation of the truth of the faith.

The moral habits of the church do not stand alone as evidence. After presenting these pieces of evidence, Aristides points to Scripture as a true and authoritative source that sustains his claim: "Take their writings and read them!" Aristides implores his readers. "You will find that I have not presented these things on my own authority" (*Apol.* 16). Nevertheless, the moral habit of valuing the vulnerable remains crucial. According to the *Apology,* the presence of the divine was demonstrated when Christians cared for widows, redeemed orphans, gave to those in need, and buried deceased believers whose families could not afford a funeral. All of this was done without public fanfare.

The practice of burying the poor is particularly noteworthy. In much of the Roman Empire, if a deceased individual could not afford burial, his or her body was tossed into a mass burial pit.[14] To avoid this fate, those with the capacity to do so joined funerary societies.[15] The bylaws of one such society were inscribed on a marble slab in Lanuvium in the year 136, during the lifetime of Aristides of Athens. Joining this funerary society required applicants to donate one hundred sestertii and one amphora of "good wine" upfront, followed by an ongoing monthly payment. The inscription on which these bylaws survive today was crafted, in part, for the purpose of publicizing the good deeds of the society's patron.[16]

The church provided a funerary society of sorts for those who

---

14 Ian Morris, *Death-Ritual and Social Structure in Classical Antiquity* (Cambridge University Press, 1992), 42.

15 Maureen Carroll, *Spirits of the Dead: Roman Funerary Commemoration in Western Europe* (Oxford University Press, 2006), 45–46.

16 The inscription is preserved by the National Museum of Rome at the Baths of Diocletian in Rome. Societies of the sort described in this inscription provided functions beyond funerary provisions; however, "the prominence of a funerary purpose in the life of Roman associations of the most varied kind is too well documented to permit marginalization." Andreas Bendlin, "Associations, Funerals, Sociality, and Roman Law: The Collegium of Diana and Antinous in Lanuvium (CIL 14.2112) Reconsidered," in *Aposteldekret und antikes Vereinswesen: Gemeinschaft und ihre Ordnung*, ed. Markus Öhler, WUNT 1.280 (Mohr Siebeck, 2011), 251–252.

could not join such societies, whether because they could not afford to do so or because the ceremonies of these societies required worship of pagan deities. Among Christians, the human body was sacred even in death, and the bodies of the poor were no less sacred than the flesh of the wealthy. Unlike the patrons of Roman funerary societies, Christians cared for the bodies of the deceased without publicizing their deeds. Christians were, in the words of Aristides, "careful that no one should notice" their charity.

Today, it is easy to read the words of Aristides and to assume that his intent was to demonstrate the value of Christianity by pointing to deeds that even non-Christians would have seen as good. After all, generosity to the poor and care for the vulnerable are likely to strike even the most hardened secularists as desirable traits today. Yet such habits were not necessarily perceived as positive traits in the larger context in which Aristides penned his *Apology*.

The Greek historian Polybius was probably exaggerating when he claimed that "no one ever thinks of giving any of his private property to anyone if he can help it."[17] Nevertheless, the writings of Lucian of Samosata reveal that generosity of the type that Aristides described was more likely to be seen as laughable than admirable in the second century.[18] A resistance to incongruous generosity was so ingrained in Roman thinking that these customs still limited people's giving long after the second century.[19] Two hundred years after Aristides, the Christian writer Lactantius caviled at Christians who hesitated to give to the poor unless there was some opportunity for honor to be bestowed or for the favor to be returned.[20]

---

17 Polybius, *The Histories*, vol. 6, *Books 28–39. Fragments*, ed. and trans. S. Douglas Olson, trans. W. R. Paton, rev. F. W. Walbank and Christian Habicht, LCL 161 (Harvard University Press, 2012), 32.12.

18 Notice in particular the sarcastic tone in chaps. 11 and 12 of "The Passing of Peregrinus" in Lucian, *The Passing of Peregrinus. The Runaways. Toxaris or Friendship. The Dance. Lexiphanes. The Eunuch. Astrology. The Mistaken Critic. The Parliament of the Gods. The Tyrannicide. Disowned,* trans. A. M. Harmon, LCL 302 (Harvard University Press, 1936).

19 The patterns of giving promoted in the writings of second-century Christians exhibit the perfection that John Barclay described as "incongruity," although "superabundance," "singularity," "priority," and "efficacy" seem to be operative as well at times. See John M. G. Barclay, *Paul and the Gift* (Eerdmans, 2015), 66–78.

20 Lactantius, *The Divine Institutes, Books I–VII*, trans. Mary Francis

Care that is incongruous with the recipients' capacity to return the favor is perceived as admirable today only because people are still mining their values from the rich moral motherlode that centuries of Christian tradition have embedded in the soil of Western civilization. Whenever secularity affirms care for the vulnerable as an act to be applauded, a system that claims to be godless is applying for a loan from the bank of the Christian tradition.

When Aristides claimed "something divine is mingled among" the people of the church after describing the church's care for the vulnerable, Aristides was not declaring that the *goodness* of these deeds demonstrated the presence of the divine among the people of the church. What he was pointing out was the *impossibility* of such counterintuitive and countercultural habits of life apart from the presence of some power that transcends every human capacity.

The ecclesial apologetic of Aristides is a transcendental argument of sorts that asks, "What else must be the case if we see an entire community of people pursuing counterintuitive and countercultural patterns of generosity?" For Aristides, the only possible response is that if a community practices generosity to the vulnerable alongside commitments such as continence, kindness, truthfulness, justice, humility, and honor for parents, then there must be "something divine mingled among them" because no community is capable of sustaining such a life without the presence and power of the divine.

2. "Those Who Hold Heretical Opinions ... Have No Concern for Love": Care for the Widow, the Orphan, and the Oppressed as a Demonstration of Orthodoxy in the Letters of Ignatius of Antioch

Sometime in the early second century, a bishop named Ignatius was sentenced to die for his faith. A contingent of ten soldiers escorted him to Rome to die. Along the way, Ignatius of Antioch

McDonald (Catholic University of America Press, 1964), 6:11. The words of Lactantius in *The Divine Institutes* 6:11 seem in some ways to hint at a non-circular ideal of giving.

penned seven letters that survive as a testament of his faith and his care for the churches.

It is Ignatius's letter to the church of Smyrna that is most relevant for this research. Speaking to the church of Smyrna against heretics who claimed that Jesus had suffered in appearance only (*Smyrn.* 2:1), Ignatius declared that anyone who makes such claims is contrary to "God's way of thinking" (γνώμη του θεού; 6:2).[21] This contrariety to the mind of God is not, however, a mere matter of thinking or believing. These heretics' disbelief in the physical sufferings of Jesus resulted in a lack of care for the physical needs that surrounded them. Those who "hold heretical opinions about the grace of Jesus Christ" are those who—according to Ignatius—also "have no concern about love, nor about the widow, nor about the orphan, nor about the oppressed, nor about the prisoner or the one released, nor about the hungry or thirsty" (6:2).

For Ignatius, wherever there is doctrinal wholeness and health, there will be living evidence of this faith embodied in the church. To believe in the physical sufferings of Jesus was to recognize some measure of continuity between the sufferings of Jesus and the sufferings of the widow, the orphan, the imprisoned, and the poor. The church enacts its Christological orthodoxy through generosity to the poor and care for the vulnerable. A lack of concern for the sufferings of the vulnerable was an outward symptom of beliefs about Jesus that were contrary to the very mind of God (6:2). The *Didache* makes a similar point, not regarding heretics with a defective Christology but regarding those who persecute Christians.[22] Ignatius extends this line of thinking to heretics who disbelieved the physical sufferings of Jesus. According to Ignatius, communities that downplay the physical sufferings of Christ become communities that fail to meet the physical needs of the vulnerable. Defective Christology results in defective care.

21 "Προς Σμυρναιους Ιγνάτιος," in *The Apostolic Fathers: Greek Texts and English Translations*, ed. and trans. Michael W. Holmes, 3rd ed. (Baker Academic, 2007), 248–261.

22 According to the *Didache,* those who persecute Christians "have no mercy for the poor, do not work on behalf of the oppressed," "turn away from those in need, oppress the afflicted, [and] advocate for the wealthy" (*Did.* 5:2). See "Διδαχή των Δώδεκα Αποστολών," in Holmes, *The Apostolic Fathers*, 344–369.

Once again, the life of the church functions as an apologetic for the reality of God's presence in his church. For Aristides of Athens, the countercultural distinctiveness of the church's care for the poor demonstrates the power of God among his people. For Ignatius of Antioch, these same acts of care are a sign of the church's confidence in the physical incarnation and sufferings of Jesus. And so, the ecclesial apologetic of care for orphans and the poor has implications not only for defending the truth of the faith but also for demonstrating a congregation's doctrinal integrity.

3. "You Will Love and Admire Those Who Suffer Punishment": Care for the Poor as Preparation for Martyrdom in Epistle to Diognetus

Epistle to Diognetus is one of the most eloquent texts from the early church. The identity of the author remains uncertain, and the date of composition is unknown. The attacks that the author counters in the treatise are typical of those leveled at the church in the mid-to-late second century; thus, the second century remains the most likely timeframe for the composition of the first ten chapters of the text.[23] These chapters reflect a time in the second century when separation between Christians and Jews was a "historical reality rather than an image, although not necessarily to the complete exclusion of the latter."[24]

The apologetic argument in *Epistle to Diognetus*—much like

---

23 Clayton Jefford, ed., *The Epistle to Diognetus (with the Fragment of Quadratus): Introduction, Text, and Commentary* (Oxford University Press, 2013); Henri Marrou, *A Diognète* (Cerf, 1952), 246–251; Henry Meecham, *The Epistle to Diognetus: The Greek Text, with Introduction, Translation, and Notes* (Manchester University Press, 1949), 16–19.

24 Florenc Mene, "Diognetus and the Parting of the Ways," *Themelios* 46, no. 2 (2021): 365. The final two chapters in the medieval manuscript from which the surviving text derives may come from a homily that is unrelated to the rest of the epistle; as such, these two chapters will not be referenced for the purposes of this research. See Bart Ehrman, ed. and trans., *The Apostolic Fathers*, vol. 2, *Epistle of Barnabas. Papias and Quadratus. Epistle to Diognetus. The Shepherd of Hermas*, LCL 25 (Harvard University Press, 2003), 124; Holmes, "The Epistle to Diognetus and the Fragment of Quadratus," in Holmes, *The Apostolic Fathers*, 689–690. For an alternative perspective on chaps. 11–12, see Charles Hill, *From the Lost*

the one in *Apology* of Aristides—extols the exemplary ethics of those who follow Jesus. Care for the parentless and the poor is not, however, emphasized in the opening chapters of the text. In the most well-known segments of the epistle, the author focuses on sexual ethics and exceptional citizenship; the church's care for the poor is mentioned only briefly and in a manner that may be metaphorical. Christians "are impoverished, yet they enrich many; they need all things, yet they abound in everything" (*Diogn.* 5:13).[25]

For the author of *Epistle to Diognetus,* the supreme evidence for the presence of divine power among the people of the church is not their morals but their martyrdoms. After describing how Christians are persecuted and even executed, the author of *Epistle to Diognetus* makes this declaration: "These things do not look like human works; they are the power of God, they are the proofs [δειγματα] of his presence [παρουσιας]" (*Diogn.* 7:9). The church's faithfulness to the point of death is the evidence of God's presence among his people.

What part, then, does care for the poor play in the apologetic argument of *Epistle to Diognetus?* In chapter 10 of the epistle, the focus turns toward an ethic that is grounded in the imitation of God. It is in this paraenetic context that the author reveals the role that care for the poor plays in the church's defense of the faith.

According to *Epistle to Diognetus,* God has revealed his benevolence toward humankind by sending Christ (10:2; see also φιλανθρωπίας; 9:2). Love for God results in imitation of God (10:4), which leads to a life that mimics God's self-giving love.[26]

Teaching of Polycarp: Identifying Irenaeus's Apostolic Presbyter and the Author of Ad Diognetum (Mohr Siebeck, 2006), 106–127.

25 Gk. Πτωχεύουσι, καὶ πλουτίζουσι πολλούς· πάντων ὑστεροῦνται, καὶ ἐν πᾶσι περισσεύουσιν. See "Προς Διογνητον," in Holmes, *The Apostolic Fathers,* 694–713.

26 The author seems to have been replying to a question that included some query related to the love of Christians for one another (φιλοστοργιαν; 1:1). The benevolent love described in 9:2 (φιλανθρωπίας; cf. Titus 3:4) suggests that the love of Christians for one another is grounded in the love of God for humanity; imitation of this love causes Christians to reach beyond love for one another and to love their neighbors who are not yet Christians. See discussion in Juan Ignacio Ruiz Aldaz, "La recepción del concepto de *philanthropía* en la literatura cristiana de los dos primeros siglos," *ScrTh* 42 (2010): 295–296.

This ethic of imitation leads Christians not to yearn for greater wealth or power because "happiness is not a matter of ... desiring to have more than weaker people, or possessing wealth and using force against one's inferiors." Hoarding of wealth and lording of power are—in the words of this epistle—"alien to the greatness" that belongs to God (10:5).

In place of a stockpile of wealth for one's own pleasure, the Christian ethic of imitation produces habits of care for the socially disadvantaged:

> Whoever takes up a neighbor's burden, whoever wishes to work for the good of someone who is worse off in something in which he himself is better off, whoever provides to those in need what he receives from God—that is the one who has received something from God. (*Diogn.* 10:6)

It is through generosity to those who are "worse off" that the people of God become God-like in the eyes of those who receive these gifts (θεός γίνεται των λαμβανόντων; 10:6) and are thereby revealed to be imitators of God. This generosity is intended to extend not only to fellow Christians but also to neighbors, regardless of whether or not these neighbors are Christians (10:5–6).[27]

It is in this context that the author reveals the apologetic function of the church's care for those who possess less. According to *Epistle to Diognetus,* those who imitate God through generosity to the poor grow to love and admire the lives of Christians who face martyrdom (10:6–7), and it is martyrdom that provides the ultimate evidence of the truthfulness of Christian faith (7:9). Habits

---

27 Although *Epistle to Diognetus* is distinctly Christian in its application, there are echoes of Stoic ideals in this exaltation of universal benevolence. The purpose of these allusions to Stoic ideals was not, however, to affirm them in their Stoic context. It was to bring readers to recognize the true, Christian meaning of these terms, which can only be understood after conversion. See Joseph Dodson, "New Friends and Old Rivals in the Letters of Seneca and *The Epistle to Diognetus,*" *PRSt* 45, no. 4 (2018): 402; Henry Meecham, *The Epistle to Diognetus,* 48–49; Michael Bird, "The Reception of Paul in the *Epistle to Diognetus,*" in *Paul and the Second Century,* ed. Michael Bird and Joseph Dodson, LNTS (T&T Clark, 2011), 71, 82, 88.

of generosity toward the powerless cultivate a heart of admiration for the persecuted, and this admiration habituates the Christian's heart to "despise that which is here esteemed to be death"; 10:7–8). A disposition of care thus prepares the believer for the possibility of his or her own martyrdom, the ultimate act of God-like generosity. To put it simply, the people of the church give their possessions to train themselves to be ready to give their lives. Care for the poor is preparation for martyrdom.

For Aristides of Athens, it is the *countercultural incongruity of the church's care for the poor that demonstrates the reality of God's presence among the people of the church.* In the letters of Ignatius, *the church's concern for physical suffering reveals the church's orthodox confidence in the reality of Jesus's physical incarnation and suffering.* For the author of *Epistle to Diognetus,* care for the poor also has an apologetic purpose, but the function is different both from the *Apology* of Aristides and from the letters of Ignatius. If I have understood *Epistle to Diognetus* rightly on this point, a life of generosity toward the poor is *a means by which God trains his people to imitate his self-giving love for humanity, even to the point of giving their lives.*

The Future of Apologetics: Better Possibilities than Proclaiming the End of Apologetics

What Myron Penner rejects in *The End of Apologetics* is any approach to apologetics that reduces hearers to rational commitments and separates the form of the argument from the content. A proper approach to apologetics in the present time seems to be, in his estimation, a post-epistemological narrative that testifies to the Word of God through the life and words of a believing community. The word of the cross embodied in the life of the church provides both the form and the content of this proclamation of the truth of Christian faith.

Part of what we see in the apologists of the second century provides much of what Penner demands. These premodern writers provided an ecclesial apologetic that saw the life of the church as evidence for the truth of the faith. Far from reducing anyone to his or her rational commitments, this apologetic was deeply embodied and communal. For Ignatius, it was precisely the church's engagement with physical needs and challenges that revealed the reality of the church's confidence in the physical sufferings of Jesus. Belief in the incarnation was distinguishable from the church's care for the orphans, the widows, and the poor; however, this living argument of concern for physical needs flowed inevitably from the church's Christology. Form and content were congruent but never collapsed.

In the *Apology* of Aristides, the witness of incongruous care for the poor revealed that "something divine" was at work among the people of the church (*Apol.* 16). And yet, this appeal to the life of the church did not prevent Aristides from appealing to rational arguments—including an aesthetic argument and a cosmological argument from motion, echoing Aristotle—to show what sort of deity the design of the cosmos necessitates. Rational apologetics and relational apologetics were not mutually exclusive in the second century. Neither did an embodied apologetic rule out appeals to the historical testimony of Scripture.

Epistle to Diognetus in particular presents us with a beautifully embodied ecclesial apologetic. A generous response to the physical needs of neighbors grows out of Christ-centered imitation of God. These acts of sacrificial generosity prepare our souls for martyrdom, the consummate evidence for the truth of our faith. A rational argument is thus made in the context of a life lived, with no reduction of the recipient to his or her rational commitments. In all of these approaches, the common ground is a pattern of generosity which the recipients cannot deny, though they might attribute it to some cause other than "something divine mingled" among the people of the church. According to *The End of Apologetics,* "what is needed in our witness, if those we engage are to be edified, is a poetics that performs the essentially Christian, in which there is no gap between the form of witness and its content."[28] And yet, what habit is more essentially Christian than practicing for martyrdom in the name of Christ? And how can the form and the content possibly be more congruent than when our

---

28 Penner, *The End of Apologetics,* 90.

preparation for death is a proclamation of his gospel through participation in his death?

Perhaps the exit doors that we're looking for are not in front of us but behind us.

Ecclesial Apologetics and the Life of the Local Church

So how might a renewed emphasis on this ecclesial apologetic strengthen how Christians in local churches proclaim the beauty of the gospel in their neighborhoods and among the nations? As I consider the church where I am privileged to serve as a pastor, three distinct truths come to mind.

1. Works of Charity Are Evidential, Not Merely Attractional

Christians seem at times to see the church's works of generosity as acts intended to attract people to church and to earn a hearing with the world, with the hope that some of these individuals might listen to the gospel. Yet the care of the church for the vulnerable is so much more than a means to attract an unbeliever's interest. *Acts of care for the socially disadvantaged are themselves evidences that "something divine" is at work in the life of the church.* This is more than a mere "lifestyle evangelism" that tries to earn a hearing through acts of charity. In ecclesial apologetics, the life of sacrificial kindness that characterizes the church is itself a confirmation of the truthfulness of the faith that the people profess. Such a life, consistently pursued by an entire community, is not merely incomprehensible but impossible apart from the suffering of Jesus and the power of his Spirit.

2. Healthy Theology Cultivates Habits of Care for the Broken and the Vulnerable

Ignatius of Antioch rightly recognized the connection between our theology and our charity. Heretics who lacked confidence in the physical incarnation and sufferings of Jesus also lacked concern for the physical sufferings that surrounded them. Of course, a pattern of care for physical needs does not guarantee a church's orthodoxy. A lack of such care, however, suggests a defect that extends beyond the church's priorities to the church's theology. If a church is hesitant to be generous to the parentless and the poor, the problem is not merely a matter of misplaced ministry priorities; this hesitance reveals a disorder in the congregation's underlying theology.

3. Preparations for Martyrdom Surround Us, and They Are Beautiful

According to the author of *Epistle to Diognetus,* generosity cultivates admiration for the persecuted and prepares us for the consummate apologetic of martyrdom. Thus, in some sense, care for the vulnerable is a dress rehearsal for dying well. It is a miniature martyrdom, a liturgy of letting go what is temporary for the sake of what is eternal. Through such generosity, Christians participate in God's self-giving love now and practice martyrdom in preparation for what may be required later.

Our churches are filled with women and men who are living out these miniature martyrdoms, and it is beautiful. The family that adopts the child whose patterns of attachment have been disordered by years of abuse, the parents who choose to raise a son with Down syndrome instead of seeking the abortion that their physician recommended, the woman who treats sex workers as human beings with dignity and helps them to forge a new life for themselves and their families, the layman who pours his life into educating penitentiary inmates who are serving life sentences, and so many others—all of these acts of incongruous generosity are participations in the cross and preparations for martyrdom, and they should drive us to whisper with Aristides, "Truly, this is a new people, and there is something divine mingled among them."

10

Dynamics of Benefaction in an Early Christian Martyrdom Narrative

Megan DeVore

PERHAPS THIS DECLARATION sounds familiar: Early Christian martyrs "profoundly unsettled the social and familial relationships on which their world had depended for its coherence."[1] At least, so insists the plentiful and otherwise quite varied scholarship on the *Passio Perpetuae et Felicitatis*.[2] The *Passio* (as it will hereafter be called) is a third-century martyr account typically remembered for the norms-eschewing antics of its clairvoyant female heroine Perpetua, who is nursing her child when not in verbal or visionary combat. This chapter counters and qualifies the sweeping assumption that normative social relationships are undone in the *Passio's* narrative. Instead, it will be advocated that the one cultural matrix in particular, that of benefaction, is of far greater importance throughout the *Passio* than has been acknowledged.

---

1 Francine Cardman, "Acts of the Women Martyrs," in *Women in Early Christianity*, ed. David Scholer, SEC 14 (Garland, 1993), 150.

2 Critical editions include Thomas Heffernan, ed., *The Passion of Perpetua and Felicity* (Oxford University Press, 2012) and C. J. M. J. van Beek, ed., *Passio Sanctarum Perpetuae et Felicitatis: Textus Graecus et Latinus* (Dekker & Van de Vegt, 1936). Translations in this chapter are my own. This assumption is replete in *Passio* assessments over the decades: e.g., W. H. C. Frend, "Blandina and Perpetua: Two Early Christian Heroines," in *Women in Early Christianity*, ed. David Scholer, SEC 14 (Garland, 1993), 87–97; Gillian Cloke, "*Mater* or Martyr: Christianity and the Alienation of Women within the Family in the Later Roman Empire," *Theology and Sexuality* 5 (1996): 37–57; Kate Cooper, "The Voice of the Victim: Gender, Representation and Early Christian Martyrdom," *BJRL* 80, no. 2 (1998): 147–157; Candida Moss, "Blood Ties: Martyrdom, Motherhood, and Family in the *Passion of Perpetua and Felicitas*," in *Women Seeking the Divine: Interdisciplinary Approaches*, ed. Stephen P. Ahearne-Kroll, James A. Kelhoffer, Paul A. Holloway, WUNT (Mohr Siebeck, 2010), 183–202.

Why is such an argument necessary? The ubiquitous emphasis on the subversive nature of the martyr act has arguably resulted in a general interpretive perception that there was a stark opposition between *secular* norms and that which was *Christian* in the current lives of the martyrs-to-be, with the latter subverting the former. While this has been challenged from other vantage points and in other texts, it still remains generally assumed with regard to the identities of the *Passio* martyrs, particularly Perpetua. The details of her social standing typically receive attention only in terms of her "background," not her present functioning.[3] Yet as Éric Rebillard, Alexander Weiß, and many others have emphasized, early Christian individuals and groups demonstrated a complex relationship with the frameworks of their socio-economic contexts and continued to operate within them in an ongoing act of cultural negotiation.[4] Inherited categories both shaped and maintained Christian realities, even as some Christian authors emphatically (perhaps too emphatically) insisted upon their alternative identity.[5] The networks of relationships and expectations of benefaction that were woven into nearly every aspect of life in antiquity are no exception.[6] Benefaction, including that of women, has received attention in numerous studies—except in readings of the *Passio.*[7]

---

3 This is not typically the case for assessment of early Christian males: e.g., the implications of Cyprian's social status are generally acknowledged to have maintained an ongoing influence over his communication.

4 Éric Rebillard, *Christians and Their Many Identities in Late Antiquity, North Africa, 200–450 CE* (Cornell University Press, 2012); Alexander Weiß, *Soziale Elite und Christentum: Studien zu ordo-Angehörigen unter den frühen Christen* (de Gruyter, 2015).

5 This can be seen, e.g., in terms of early Christian use of the language and model of Greco-Roman associations: cf. Philip Harland, *Dynamics of Identity in the World of the Early Christians* (T&T Clark, 2009).

6 The general tendencies of patronage and benefaction (or euergetism) are often difficult to distinguish from one another, particularly during the Roman imperial era; I follow standard terms as nuanced to context as possible but often interchangeably in the face of indistinguishability. See Zeba Crook, *Reconceptualising Conversion: Patronage, Loyalty, and Conversion in the Religions of the Ancient Mediterranean* (Walter de Gruyter, 2004), 59–66; J. H. Elliott, "Patronage and Clientism in Early Christian Society: A Short Reading Guide," *Forum* 3, no. 4 (1987): 39–48.

7 Theresa J. Calpino, *Women, Work, and Leadership in Acts,* WUNT 2.361

This chapter advocates that the *Passio* is actually quite normal in that it is replete with the vocabularies of benefaction. After a concise sketch of how the text depicts Perpetua's socio-economic position, pertinent contemporary parameters of benefaction will be briefly reviewed. Then, a few instances in the text where sensitivity to this paradigm are highlighted. This will lead ultimately to a horizon of interpretive implications for not only this text but for studies in Antiquity and Early Christianity in general.

A brief review of the *Passio* is first in order. The account describes the martyrdom of six Christians in Carthage at the dawn of the third century. Its authorship is particularly intriguing in that it claims to be multi-vocal: it features an introduction evidently composed somewhat soon after the account's events, cast for a liturgical setting by an anonymous author typically called the "redactor" or "principal narrator."[8] The text then introduces selective and somewhat unusual narratives authored from prison by two of the text's own characters. The principal narrative voice subsequently returns with a novel-esque description of the group's martyrdom in an amphitheater, focusing predominantly on Perpetua, and concludes with a final exhortation focused on shaping the audience's collective memory.

After this review, it is necessary to alight on several key sections

---

(Mohr Siebeck, 2014); Lynn Cohick, *Women in the World of the Earliest Christians* (Baker Academic, 2009); Emily Hemelrijk, *Hidden Lives, Public Personae: Women and Civic Life in the Roman West* (Oxford University Press, 2015); Katherine Bain, *Women's Socioeconomic Status and Religious Leadership in Asia Minor: In the First Two Centuries C.E.* (Fortress, 2014). Recent work on the *Acts of Paul and Thecla*, too, has emphasized that patronage has been inadequately acknowledged as a significant presence in the plot of the text: cf. Magda Misset-van de Weg, "A Wealthy Woman Named Tryphaena: Patroness of Thecla of Iconium," in *The Apocryphal Acts of Paul and Thecla*, ed. Jan Bremmer (Pharos, 1996), 17–35.

8 The phraseology is liturgical and technically appropriate only for one bearing some authority within a Christian community, such as a bishop or presbyter. The audience is addressed as "brothers and children," for example, and the many words for reading and hearing (e.g., *lectione, audivimus, per auditum, legere*) imply an aural intention for the account. While this could suggest that the redactor was none other than the benevolent bishop Pomponius mentioned throughout the *Passio*, e.g., 3.7, 6.7, 10.1, the redactor's identity and role ultimately remain unknown.

in the narrative. Firstly, after the initial sweeping prologue, the voice
of the principal narrator provides an introduction to the *Passio's*
main characters with an intriguing description: "a group of adolescent catechumens were apprehended: Revocatus and his fellow
slave Felicitas, Saturninus and Secundulus" (2.1.1).[9] Then, another
figure is singled out with a curious cadence of phrases that echo
the contemporary style of an epigraph[10]: "Among them was Vibia
Perpetua, nobly born, abundantly educated, honorably married"
(2.1.2). It is she, the narrator continues, who *reliquit*, "bequeaths,"
the following account. This highly crafted introduction of Perpetua's social background, like other intermittent remarks throughout
the text, gesture explicitly to her noble standing and deeds. As the
only figure in the work given a familial *nomen*, Vibia, Perpetua's
comparatively high social standing is accentuated, as many have
discussed.[11] The term "nobly born" generally refers to those of sen-
atorial or decurial status, and, indeed, no less than three Carthaginian proconsuls during the recent century bore the Vibii name.
In addition, the phrase "of an honourable [noble] marriage" typically serves as a signifier of a Roman female's dignity and family
networks.[12] It would appear that the family Perpetua was born into

---

9 The term "adolescent" is vague in the Roman imperial era and can refer to
between approximately 12 and 26 years of age.

10 E.g., *CIL* VIII.870, with *matronaliter nupta* and an abbreviated *honestae
memoriae femina*.

11 Jan Bremmer, "Perpetua and Her Diary: Authenticity, Family, and Visions," in *Martyrer und Martyrerakten*, ed. Walter Ameling (Franz Steiner Verlag,
2002), 86–95, comments extensively on the Vibii and their social standing. Perpetua should have been exempt from such legal punishment due to this standing;
on the abnormal policies of Hilarianus, cf. James Rives, "Piety of a Persecutor,"
JECS 4, no. 1 (1996): 1–25. Why would an elite Roman matron be nursing her
own infant, as Perpetua does in the account? Though it may at first seem ques-
tionable, there was actually little contemporary consensus on whether the milk of
a wet-nurse or the mother would more preferably impact the child's future. Favorinus argued vigorously that well-born women ought to nurse their offspring,
and contemporary depictions confirm that breast-milk was seen as nourishment
to the intellect and character (Favorinus's view is preserved in Aulus Gellius,
Noct. Att. 12.1.20). Additionally, if Felicitas was a slave in Perpetua's *domus*, she
may well have been intended as *nutrix* for Perpetua's child once she herself gave
birth.

12 E.g., *CIL* VIII.870.

was thoroughly Romanized, seeped in civic responsibility and its corollary honours, connections—and benefaction.

Set as they were within a wider framework of norms, these pervasive relationships of reciprocity served, in Seneca's definition, as "the foremost bond of society."[13] Even as the ramifications of benefaction reached into the public realm, its function was rooted ultimately in the household.[14] Within benefaction's layered arenas of influence and relationship, we find a system that was ideally magnanimous yet decidedly reciprocal. Interactions were vertical, asymmetrical, and could be collective or individual; they were also tiered, with ascending levels of support regarded as reaching to divine realms. According to Seneca, the "benefits" of benefaction included money, various provisions, social connections, legal support or influence, advice, and "assistance from the gods"; recipients were informally bound to certain obligations, most prominently various forms of public expression denoting gratitude via flattering honorary remembrance for the deeds of the benefactor.[15] Here we are reminded of Ramsey MacMullen's key claim: in the Roman world, power depended "on perceptions, on symbols and gestures."[16] That is, power was decidedly on display, and benefaction corroborated in the constant, coded parade.

While these expressions of gratitude often took place in honorific inscriptions, statues, and monuments in public spaces,[17]

---

13 Seneca, *Ben.* 1.4.2.

14 Patronage and benefaction are acknowledged as the primary mechanism for the allocation of resources as well as for the connection between the (so-called) public and private. Cf. Katheryn Lomas and Tim Cornell, *'Bread and Circuses': Euergetism and Municipal Patronage in Roman Italy* (Routledge, 2003), 1–24; Paul Veyne, *Bread and Circuses: Historical Sociology and Political Pluralism* (Penguin, 1992), 362.

15 Seneca, *Ben.* 1.2.4; e.g., the reciprocity seen throughout Apuleius's *Metam.*; cf. Elliott, "Patronage," 39–48; Crook, *Reconceptualising Conversion*, 56–58.

16 Ramsay MacMullen, "Personal Power in the Roman Empire," *AJP* 107 (1986): 512–524.

17 Christian Witschel, "The Public Presence of Women in the Cities of Roman North Africa. Two Case Studies: Thamugadi and Cuicul," in *Women and the Roman City in the Latin West*, ed. Emily Hemelrijk and Greg Woolf (Brill, 2013), 87; Ramsay MacMullen, "Women in Public in the Roman Empire," *Historia* 29 (1980): 208–218.

patrons did not necessarily rely on their clients for the honor: self-commemoration on a grand public scale is frequently attested in self-funded inscriptions and *ante mortem* tombs and monuments[18]—relatively secure means to ensure the endurance of a constructed memory after death.[19] The quintessential examples of this with Eumachia of Pompeii[20] reminds us that Roman women had long set such trends in public acts of benefaction and commemoration, and that from the first century to the early third century, an ever-steady increase in such activity among females is evident.[21] This coincides with other developments, as elite daughters married both later in life and *sine manu*, maintaining unprecedented legal capacities.[22] They exerted significant economic power, leaving a public mark on their communities; such relationships

18 See, e.g., Stine Birk, *Depicting the Dead: Self-Representation and Commemoration on Roman Sarcophagi with Portraits*, Aarhus Studies in Mediterranean Antiquity 11 (Aarhus University Press, 2013).

19 E.g., *CIL* X.810–813; *CIL* X.292; Alison Cooley, "Women beyond Rome: Trend-Setters or Dedicated Followers of Fashion?" in *Women and the Roman City in the Latin West*, ed. Emily Hemelrijk and Greg Woolf (Brill, 2013), 23–46; Emily Hemelrijk, "Female Munificence in the Cities of the Latin West," in *Women and the Roman City in the Latin West*, ed. Emily Hemelrijk and Greg Woolf (Brill, 2013), 65–84.

20 *CIL* X.810; *CIL* X.813. In her name we have the funding of a public passageway (on the east side of the forum, no less!) complete with a self-commemorative inscription and a nod to her own divine patrons, as well as a massive *ante mortem* tomb and a dedicatory statue placed by a local association in return for her patronage. Her funding of a public passageway is noted in an inscription on one of its walls. Its words indicate her honor, her legacy, and her divine dedicatees, who then feature as her own benefactors and highlight her connected status: "Eumachia, daughter of Lucius, public priestess, in her own name and that of her son, Marcus Numistrius Fronto, built with her own funds the porch, covered passage, and colonnade and dedicated them to Concordia Augusta and to Pietas." The largest extant tomb in Pompeii was her commission, built "for herself and for her own [household]" (*sibi et suis*). Lastly, a public statue (located now in the Museo Nazionale, Naples), dedicated by an association of clients, portrays her as a pious civic priestess; it bears an inscription largely repeating her own: "To Eumachia, daughter of Lucius, public priestess, the fullers [dedicate this statue]." Cooley, "Women beyond Rome," 23–46; Cohick, *Women in the World*, 296.

21 MacMullen, "Women in Public," 210.

22 Hemelrijk, "Female Munificence," 70; Brent Shaw, "The Age of Roman Girls at Marriage: Some Reconsiderations," *JRS* 77 (1987): 38. This includes property, inheritance, and legal responsibility for children.

and actions integrated women into the public realm and offered a direct avenue to *dignitas*.[23] Benefaction, as Emily Hemelrijk concludes, "changed the notion of exemplary womanhood" during the first centuries CE.[24]

To focus in on Perpetua's Roman North Africa, an average of 29 percent of all inscriptions related to benefaction indicate a woman as the source of giving.[25] Approximately 90 percent of these are funerary and honorific, indicating a tendency for both self-commemoration *and* highly stylized honor from recipients only situated around the benefactor's death.[26] Such gestures might be obvious carved in stone, but what of literary venues that honor benefactors? Here, benefactory roles are not as overt. The example of Ummidia Quadratilla, a woman of consular rank in the late first century CE, illustrates this precisely. In one of his self-published letters (*Ep.* 7.24), Pliny the Younger sets forth an obituary in her memory. Though he calls her a "leading lady" (*princeps femina*) and includes in the letter a brief catalogue of her various traits and deeds, as well as panegyric typical for a benefactress, he never *directly* indicates her benefactory roles or relationships. Inscriptions from her hometown, however, confirm that this was precisely the case: she funded the building of a temple and an amphitheater, paid for the repairs of a theatre, and sponsored several public banquets in acts of overt munificence.[27] In such instances, keyed vocabularies

---

23 Hemelrijk and Woolf, eds., introduction to *Women and the Roman City in the Latin West* (Brill, 2013), 2–3; Kathryn McDonnell, "A Gendered Landscape: Roman Women's Monuments, Patronage, and Urban Contexts in Pompeii, Isola Sacra, and Aquileia" (PhD diss., University of North Carolina at Chapel Hill, 2005), 19–35.

24 Hemelrijk, "Female Munificence," 80.

25 Tabulated by Witschel, cited in Hemelrijk, "Female Munificence," 69. Cf. Hemelrijk and Woolf, eds., introduction to *Women and the Roman City*, 1–5; Francesca Cenerini, "The Role of Women as Municipal *Matres*," in *Women and the Roman City in the Latin West*, ed. Emily Hemelrijk and Greg Woolf (Brill, 2013), 9–22; Hemelrijk, "Female Munificence," 65–84; MacMullen, "Women in Public," 208–218. In the wider Roman empire, most scholars estimate that one-tenth of all benefactors and patrons were women.

26 Witschel, "Public Presence of Women," 85–106; Hemelrijk, *Hidden Lives, Public Personae*, 301.

27 *CIL* X.5183; cf. Hemelrijk, "Female Munificence," 65–66.

such as *gratia* implicitly indicate benefactory affiliations.[28] Can we extend this to the literature of Christians?

To begin, as has been abundantly documented,[29] the role of wealthy female benefactors was significant in the development and maintenance of Christian communities in the first centuries.[30] Contemporaneously to the *Passio*, Tertullian's vocabularies assume the paradigms of Roman *beneficia*, even as he attempts to downplay the pervasive socio-economic differences among Christians.[31] Tertullian (ever the pugilist) also complains of Christian women in Carthage who are "puffed up by their matron title"[32]; he expresses concern that these aristocratic women are still maintaining

---

28 See Richard Saller, "Status and Patronage," in *The High Empire, A.D. 70-192*, ed. Alan K. Bowman, Peter Garnsey, and Dominic Rathbone, CAH 11 (Cambridge University Press, 2000), 838-839, and *Personal Patronage under the Early Empire* (Cambridge University Press, 1982), 145-194, which explores the extensive patronage terminologies, networks, and expectations in Roman North Africa specifically. See also Miriam Griffin, "*De Beneficiis* and Roman Society," *JRS* 93 (2003): 92-113; Barbara Gold, "'The Master Mistress of My Passion': The Lady as Patron in Ancient and Renaissance Literature," in *Woman's Power, Man's Game: Essays on Classical Antiquity in Honor of Joy K. King*, ed. Mary DeForest (Bolchazy-Carducci, 1993), 284, which summarizes the extensive epigraphical evidence for many prominent wealthy women actively engaged in the public life of their Roman communities via benefaction during the early imperial era.

29 E.g., Rufina of Smyrna, whose tomb inscription identifies her as a Jewess and *archisynagogista*; Veturia Paula, a convert to Judaism, is called the "mother" of two synagogues in cities just outside of Rome ("mother" is used throughout the Greco-Roman world during the first three centuries to denote a benefactory and functional civic or religious role, one not indicating actual maternal/marital status). See Bernadette Brooten, "Female Leadership in the Ancient Synagogue," in *From Dura to Sepphoris: Studies in Jewish Art and Society in Late Antiquity*, ed. L. Levine and Z. Weiss, JRASup 40 (Journal of Roman Archaeology, 2000), 215-223; Cohick, *Women in the World*, 210-216.

30 Authors of New Testament texts, Hermas, Irenaeus, and myriad others indicate support provided by elite women; see, e.g., Luke 8:3; Irenaeus, *Haer.* 1.13.4-7; see also Alistair Stewart-Sykes, "Ordination Rites and Patronage Systems in Third Century Africa," *VC* 56 (2002): 115-130.

31 E.g, Tertullian, *Apol.* 39.1; Dennis Groh, "Upper-Class Christians in Tertullian's Africa: Some Observations," StPatr 14 (1976): 41-47; Harry Maier, *The Social Setting of the Ministry as Reflected in the Writings of Hermas, Clement and Ignatius* (Wilfrid Laurier University Press, 1991), 118. Cf. Stewart-Sykes, "Ordination Rites," 115-128.

32 Tertullian, *Ux.* 2.8.3.

their civic roles "out of the obligations of wealth, birth, and former dignities."[33] It is worth asking then, why *Passio* studies so consistently view social status as something Perpetua the revolutionary *renounced* (or does not actually have) upon claiming a Christian identity, rather than participates and negotiates within still, even as a Christian. This chapter voices that very question, and now moves to expose and examine a few instances of where the conspicuous ethos of benefaction seems to manifest in the *Passio*, emphasizing how this might affect a reading of the text.

Relatively early in Perpetua's narrative (4.1), she is given a petition from one of her fellow Christian prisoners: "Then my brother said to me, 'Lady sister, already you are so greatly honored, so much so that you might demand a vision and it might be shown to you whether there will be a martyrdom or a freedom to go forth—that is, a discharge.'" It is not surprising that interpreters perceive this exchange in a variety of ways, but it is surprising that none suggest the encoded language of benefaction. This section is most often read as a reflection of the presumption that confessors, as martyrs-to-be, possessed the ability to receive and transmit divine information.[34] However, as is revealed in the question itself and in

---

33 Tertullian, *Cult. fem.* 2.9.4, 2.11.2–3. As I have suggested elsewhere with regard to a circle of literate female exegetes receiving Tertullian's literary wrath for their interpretation of the Thecla narrative, it certainly ought to be considered (but heretofore has not been) that Perpetua numbers among this group of elite Christian women that Tertullian writes polemic *against*. For further information on Christianity in Carthage during this period, see Jane Merdinger, "Roman North Africa," in *Early Christianity in Contexts*, ed. William Tabbernee (Baker Academic, 2014), 233–235; J. Patout Burns and Robin Jensen, *Christianity in Roman Africa* (Eerdmans, 2014), 1–7; William Tabbernee estimates that there were twelve hundred Christians at most in Carthage. William Tabbernee, "To Pardon or not to Pardon: North African Montanism and the Forgiveness of Sins," *StPatr* 36 (2001): 375–386. But Keith Hopkins avers that there were between five and ten thousand. Keith Hopkins, "Christian Number and Its Implications," *JECS* 6, no. 2 (1998): 202.

34 Tertullian even considered it necessary to critique Carthaginian Christians' superfluous praise and perception of potency for confessors; he acerbically remarks that confessors are "swarmed" in prison by those making a "plea for prayers" (*Pud.* 22). Notwithstanding Tertullian's slight tendency to hyperbole, his remarks not only display the common perception of a heightened spiritual status of confessors—seemingly somewhat comparable to spiritual benefactors—but

the surrounding narrative, the imprisoned group has not yet been formally tried—no one is yet a confessor. Furthermore, since the "brother" is a fellow prisoner, is he not on the same spiritual level of "proto-confessorship" as Perpetua? Other interpreters argue she is the prophetess of the group – so the account is a product of an early circle of the New Prophecy (Montanism), with Perpetua as oracle.[35] Attention to the deferential, socially encoded question, however, provides another explanation.

In this world, a liaison between benefactor and recipient typically followed a formulaic code, or scripting. First, the recipient delivered a formal *salutatio* accompanied by reverent praise; a specific request then followed via a transitional statement specifically honoring the patron with gratitude for the patron's privileged social status which would enable the request to be fulfilled.[36] We see

---

also are interesting in that he specifically locates this practice among non-Montanist Christians in Carthage with whom he prefers to disassociate himself. A vivid contemporary example of the potency of confessors is Blandina in *Mart. Lyons*, who converses in a familiar way with Christ (ὁμιλία πρός χριστόν). Not only is this evident in early traditions, such as with Stephen (who beholds "the glory of God and the Son of Man at God's right hand" immediately after delivering a resounding apology to a sizeable audience in Acts 7:1–56), but Cyprian's mid-third-century epistles also present confessors as spiritual exemplars and prophetic voices; see Cyprian, *Epistle* 8 (*ANF* vol. 5), where the confessor-martyr Mappalicus prophetically utters to the proconsul interrogating him, "You shall see a contest tomorrow."; Origen's *Exhortation to Martyrdom* 2 portrays confessor-martyrs as those who experience God's "multiplied benefits and favors." Andrew McGowan explains, "The capacity of the martyrs to inhabit and make present the example of Christ added a heavenly structure to the Roman world's patronage system." Andrew McGowan, *Ancient Christian Worship: Early Church Practices in Social, Historical, and Theological Perspective* (Baker Academic, 2014), 243. Here, according to Joyce Salisbury, the brother assumes that Perpetua could serve as a visionary intermediary because she "has been selected for martyrdom," in *Perpetua's Passion: The Death and Memory of a Young Roman Woman* (New York: Routledge, 1997), 98.

35 See useful summary of this position in Christoph Markschies, "The *Passio Sanctarum Perpetuae et Felicitatis* and Montanism?," in *Perpetua's Passions: Multidisciplinary Approaches to the* Passio Perpetuae et Felicitatis, ed. Jan Bremmer and Marco Formisano (Oxford University Press, 2012), 277–290. The two most prominent studies promoting this claim are Heffernan, ed., *Passion*, and Rex Butler, *The New Prophecy and 'New Visions': Evidence of Montanism in the Passion of Perpetua and Felicitas* (Catholic University Press of America, 2006).

36 Seneca, *Ben.* 2.24.4; also in Horace, *Sat.* 1.1.9–10; see Crook,

this formulaic appeal in the contemporary *Metamorphoses* (11.2), where Apuleius's Lucius makes an invocation to Isis in an albeit more long-winded fashion: he greets her with an honorable identification, praises her status, then makes his request.[37] The process is duplicated in the *Passio*: we see the distinctive deferential title *domina*,[38] then the subsequent *soror*, which reinforces the relationship of reciprocity as consistent with the encoded language of associations, household networks, and early Christian communities.[39] The request is crafted with the requisite obsequious (and unoriginal) praise: Perpetua is "great in honor," a stock formula indicating *dignitas* and one explicitly classified by Seneca as *the* appropriate compliment in relationships of benefaction.[40] The content of the brother's appeal, that Perpetua might request a vision and be shown the upcoming fate of the imprisoned company, also echoes Seneca's catalogue of benefits potentially requested—advice from the divine realm.[41] Perpetua's response then confirms this encoded, tiered, vertical relationship: she agrees to the request because "I knew I could speak with the Lord, whose *beneficia* I myself had

---

Reconceptualising Conversion, 71–72, 119.

37   This is not exclusive to the secular realm, e.g., 2 Cor 4:15; 8:4. "Benefit," "favor" or "beneficence" can all be considered equivalents of χάρις within the Graeco-Roman social system. For a useful discussion of the term χάρις, or grace, see Crook, *Reconceptualising Conversion,* 132–150. Use of the term precedes the Roman era; e.g., Herodotus mentions Pausianus's request for archers from Athens as a χάρις (*Hist.* 9.60.3).

38   This term quite likely indicates that she is the mistress of a household, as seen in the likes of Cicero, Quintilian, Virgil, Propertius, the *Vetus Latina,* and the later Vulgate. The small handful of "exceptions" are ironic, like "mistress of my passion" (Ovid, *Am.* 2.16), and ultimately still reveal degrees of deference and authority.

39   Cf. Harland, *Dynamics of Identity,* 63–96. E.g., *P.Oxy.* 63 4365, which contains the address of an anonymous letter writer in Upper Egypt: the sender greets the female recipient, whom Haines-Eitzen postulates was the owner of a library, as "lady sister in the Lord" and makes a request, in Kim Haines-Eitzen, *The Gendered Palimpsest: Women, Writing, and Representation in Early Christianity* (Oxford University Press, 2012), 33; see also AnneMarie Luijendijk, *Greetings in the Lord: Early Christians and the Oxyrhynchus Papyri,* HTS 60 (Harvard Divinity School, 2008), 70–74.

40   Seneca, *Ben.* 7.22; cf. Apuleius, *Metam.* 5.19.1, 5.12.15, 11.1–11.4.

41   Seneca, *Ben.* 1.2; cf. J. H. Elliott, "Patronage," 39–48; Crook, *Reconceptualising Conversion,* 56–58.

already abundantly experienced."[42] I contend what is occurring in this passage, then, is that Perpetua is receiving a request from a recipient who already views her as a social intermediary. The impact of the mechanisms of *beneficia* are illuminating, and less tenable exegetical options are no longer required (as creative as they may be).

Another example includes the perplexingly-occasional second female in the narrative: Felicitas, introduced as a slave. Perpetua's own account never once mentions her, but the principal narrator's account does, notably in a focused depiction of her incarcerated birth experience as a "kindness of the Lord." It is useful here to recall Keith Bradley's striking summary that "marginality and pseudo-invisibility characterized representations" of slaves in contemporary literary, inscriptional, and epigraphic sources.[43] That is, when contemporary honorific sources feature slaves, they are passively but dutifully placed in task on the margins of the scene in miniature below the protagonist: the public depiction of the fidelity of slaves was a nod of honor to their owners.[44] If Felicitas is

---

42 A metacritical aside may be exigent here. Nearly a century earlier, Tacitus had transformed Livia's patronage into a quintessential picture of sinister female domination. A powerfully benevolent woman found no room, it seems, in Tacitaean paradigms. Perhaps the same might be said of Perpetua: typical commentary has dictated that if a female seems to be exercising any kind of authority, this authority is not actually her own. It must stem from the chrism of oracular prophecy, one in which she is more of a vessel, rather than from sources that belong to her and are socially legitimate. This is an implication of interpretations which consider Perpetua to be a Montanist.

43 Even among those who "acknowledged the humanity of the slaves," slaves were not encouraged to "develop their character in any independent, self-fulfilling fashion." Keith Bradley, *Slavery and Society at Rome* (University of Cambridge Press, 1994), 140; Bain, *Women's Socioeconomic Status*, 53–54.

44 Concentration on Christians as revolutionaries has resulted in inadequate acknowledgement that there is little evidence that the lives of household slaves changed for those in early Christian households: see discussion in Cohick, *Women in the World*, 260–263; Heffernan, ed., *Passion*, 18–21. See examples and discussion in Bain, *Women's Socioeconomic Status*, 137–168, which discusses female slaves, religious status, and socioeconomic status; cf. Natalie Kampen, *Image and Status: Roman Working Women in Ostia* (Gebr. Mann, 1981), 131; Marice Rose, "The Construction of Mistress and Slave Relationships in Late Antique Art," *Woman's Art Journal* 29, no. 2 (2008): 41–49. Cf. discussion in Jennifer A. Glancy, *Slavery in Early Christianity* (Fortress, 2006), 11–12: in a third-century

Perpetua's slave, possibly one intended to be *nutrix* for Perpetua's infant son, then the redactor's explicit declaration that Felicitas received a favor of kindness from the Lord (15.1) would be heard as a participation in the vertically-ascending layers of patronage and the household, using again the scripted *gratia* language of benefactory giving. Thus, Felicitas's quite brief moments in the narrative, in the margins of the scene in miniature below the protagonist, both in her own pericope and in the depiction of the amphitheater's events, can be seen as a literary "margin," a nod as much to (or perhaps more to) Perpetua.

Another striking confirmation of the matrices of benefaction in the text occurs at the point in the *Passio* as the redactor's authorial voice resumes in the latter portion of the work and begins the account of the martyrdom itself. Here, a direct address to the audience abruptly interrupts the narrative: "The Spirit has allowed and thus willed" the account of these events[45] to be written, and "we will carry out the mandate [*mandatum*], or really the sacred commission [*fideicommissum*], of the *most holy* Perpetua" (16.1). The redactor's trifold employment of overtly rhetorical constructs, the *lingua* of a commission and command, and nearly-hyperbolic humility and praise is an exactly standard case within the mores of commemoration for a benefactor.[46] The *inclusio* rhetoric portrays the redactor and his audience as together being faithful to the will of the Spirit by passing down this account,[47] validating and even

---

legal petition, for example, a female slaveowner laments that the kidnapping of one of her slaves is an act of violence against herself. Glancy also argues that in a variety of contexts, including legal situations, slaves functioned as "body-doubles" for their owners.

45 *Munus* is typically reserved for aspects of benefaction done out of civic ambition. While it can specifically refer to a public spectacle offered by a civic magistrate (e.g., Suetonius, *Tit.* 7), it can invoke any kind of tribute, duty, favor, service, or obligatory gift (e.g., Cicero, *Sen.* 11.35; Nepos, *Thras.* 4.2; synonyms for *munus* are, in fact, *officium*, *honos*, and *ministerium*). To what *munus* is the narrator referencing?

46 See discussion in Griffin, "*De Beneficiis* and Roman Society," 92–113, which explores the style of discourse and the technique of hyperbole in the language of reciprocity.

47 We see this rhetorical technique in Josephus: he claims that when he presented his *Jewish War* to Vespasian and Titus, Titus "mandated that they be

divinely mandating *Perpetua's* own commission. The seemingly redundant use of *fideicommissum* is notable, since it is an explicitly legal term for an obligatory trust or bequest given to one person but to be delivered to a third party, managing the processes of the distribution of property after death in accordance with the personal direction of the deceased.[48] The *Passio* narrator's language here, then, is tantalizing. Could it confirm that the account itself, including the section voiced by Perpetua, originates within the broader realities of benefaction? It is justifiable to say that this may be precisely the case.

Based on merely these brief examples from different points in the *Passio*, significant implications can be proposed. Most broadly, the pervasive assumption that the *Passio* martyrs entirely disrupted the social norms and relationships that had comprised their world has arguably resulted in a lacuna that has impacted interpretation. Instead of viewing Perpetua's elite identity as part of her "pre-conversion" background, this chapter has suggested that her social status ought to be viewed as a formative and functional reality throughout the narrative, impacting both content and genre. The common critique of the narrator's enthusiasm for Perpetua may simply fail to acknowledge the genre in which he seems to be participating.[49] While his panegyric has prompted most commentators to express hermeneutical suspicion,[50] such a view possibly neglects the interlaced gearworks of *beneficium* and the ide-

published" (*Vita* 361–363).

48 See Quintilian, *Inst.* 9.2.74; Gaius, *Inst.* 2.184; Suetonius, *Claud.* 23; Ulpian, *Frag.* 29.1. Cf. A. Watson, *The Law of Succession in the Later Roman Republic* (Oxford University Press, 1977), 35; Ville Vuolanto, "Women and the Property of Fatherless Children in the Roman Empire," in *Women, Wealth, and Power in the Roman Empire*, by P. Setälä, R. Berg, R. Hälikkä, M. Keltanen, J. Pölönen, V. Vuolanto (Institutum Romanum Finlandiae, 2002), 227.

49 Numerous studies have focused upon the modern failure to understand the pedagogic technique of hyperbole in antiquity: see discussion in Griffin, "*De Beneficiis* and Roman Society," 92–113, which explores the style of discourse and the pedagogic technique of hyperbole in the language of reciprocity. Cf. also MacMullen, "Personal Power in the Roman Empire," 512–524.

50 E. R. Dodds, *Pagan and Christian in an Age of Anxiety: Some Aspects of Religious Experience from Marcus Aurelius to Constantine* (Cambridge University Press, 1965), 49.

alizing that occurred in public commemoration for benefactors. Aspects of benefaction manifesting in the account are especially significant in at least three scenarios at different points in the text, each involving "gifts" or "grace." When the vocabularies and realities of the contextual landscapes of benefaction are attended, otherwise peculiar or incongruous aspects of the *Passio* narrative are given new perspective. Lastly, the *Passio* may provide another valuable window into female munificence in antiquity, contributing to broader scholarship on early Christian benefaction and the socio-economic dynamics at play in the second and third century church in its Greco-Roman milieu. This certainly warrants further pursuit.

Index

9 781948 048736